THE TENT OF
ABRAHAM

THE TENT OF ABRAHAM

*Stories of Hope and Peace for
Jews, Christians, and Muslims*

JOAN CHITTISTER, OSB

MURSHID SAADI SHAKUR CHISHTI

RABBI ARTHUR WASKOW

FOREWORD BY KAREN ARMSTRONG

BEACON PRESS, BOSTON

Beacon Press
25 Beacon Street
Boston, Massachusetts 02108-2892
www.beacon.org

Beacon Press books
are published under the auspices of
the Unitarian Universalist Association of Congregations.

11 10 09 08 07   8 7 6 5 4 3 2 1

This book is printed on acid-free paper that meets the uncoated paper
ANSI/NISO specifications for permanence as revised in 1992.

Text design by Bob Kosturko
Composition by Wilsted & Taylor Publishing Services

Chittister, Joan.
    The tent of Abraham : stories of hope and peace for Jews, Christians,
and Muslims / Joan Chittister, Saadi Shakur Chishti (Neil Douglas-Klotz),
Arthur Waskow ; foreword by Karen Armstrong.
        p. cm.
    ISBN 978-0-8070-7729-0 (pbk. : alk. paper) 1. Abraham (Biblical
patriarch) 2. Christianity. 3. Judaism. 4. Islam. I. Douglas-Klotz, Neil.
II. Waskow, Arthur Ocean III. Title.

BS580.A3C45 2006
222'.11092—dc22   2006001274

To Dena Merriam,
in gratitude for her global vision and her
persistent commitment to the spirituality of peacemaking,
and to the
Reverend Joan Brown Campbell,
in recognition of her unending determination
to raise the public voice of women everywhere.

—JC

For Murshid Shamcher Beorse and Haji Shemseddin Ahmed,
who worked tirelessly for the common good
of all the children of Adam and Eve.

—SSC

To honor Vincent Harding, sage,
Zalman Schachter-Shalomi, rabbi of deep ecumenism,
and
Father David Gracie, priest and prophet.

—AW

CONTENTS

FOREWORD

Abraham: Meeting Guests, Meeting God

KAREN ARMSTRONG

THE STORY OF ABRAHAM, EXPLORED HERE BY THE AUTHORS from the Christian, Muslim, and Jewish perspectives, is a story of pluralism that is sorely needed in this time of religious hatred. In the Christian tradition, Abraham is often called the father of those who believe, but he has none of the hard certainties of dogmatic faith. Instead, the Bible repeatedly shows Abraham in the dark, asking questions of God and getting remarkably unsatisfactory answers. At a time when we have seen too much certainty, *The Tent of Abraham* reminds us that the kind of confusion, fear, and dismay that so many of us are experiencing can be the start of a new religious quest.

Yet Abraham did have one luminous encounter. Genesis 18 tells us that one day while he was sitting outside his tent at Mamre in the broiling heat of a Middle Eastern afternoon, he saw three strangers on the horizon. Strangers in the ancient world were potentially lethal people, because they were not bound by the local laws of vendetta and could strike with impunity. Even today, very few of us would invite three total strangers off the street and into our own home. But that is what Abraham did. He ran out eagerly to meet these people, who did not belong to his ethnic or religious group. The text emphasizes his haste: he is not dragging his feet, approaching these travelers with reluctance, but runs out to greet them, prostrating himself before them as though they were kings. He then tells his wife to prepare an elaborate meal to refresh them during their arduous journey. And during the ensuing conversation, it transpires quite naturally that one of these strangers is Abraham's God. The act of practical compassion led directly to a divine encounter.

This is a strange story to find in a Jewish scripture, because later Jewish teaching would be wary of seeing the divine in human form. But it expresses a religious truth found in all the major traditions: it is compassion, not righteousness and doctrinal certainty, that leads us into the presence of what monotheists call God but others have termed Nirvana, Brahman, or the Tao. Greek Orthodox Christians have always loved this story, regarding it as an early manifestation of God as Trinity. A famous icon by the fifteenth-century painter Andrei Rublev depicts the three travelers as angels, representing Father, Word, and Holy Spirit, and has transformed Abraham's meal into the Eucharist. The message is clear: the mysterious revelation of the Trinity will only make sense in the context of the liturgy and of generous communion with our fellow human beings, all of whom are sacred emissaries.

It is of the utmost importance that Abraham's three visitors were strangers. In Hebrew, the word *qadosh* (holy) means "separate, other." It is the otherness of the stranger —even perhaps the initial recoil that we may feel when confronted with people who seem alien—that can give us intimations of the holiness of God. Religion was implicated in the catastrophe of September 11. Monotheists must reclaim their traditions from murderous sectarianism and return to the compassion that is the core of their faith.

Muhammad understood this very well. When he made the hijra from Mecca to Medina in 622, he was excited about the prospect of working alongside the Jewish tribes there. But some of the Jews refused to accept Muhammad as a prophet, and Muhammad also learned that Jews and Christians, whom he had understood to belong to one religion—the religion of the one God—had serious theological differences, and had split the faith into warring sects. This seemed reprehensible to Muhammad, who turned more and more toward Abraham. Living before the Torah and the Gospel, Abraham was neither a Jew nor a Christian but represented a simpler faith that reflected the unity of God.

The friendly Jews of Medina had told Muhammad that the Arabs were descended from Ishmael, the son of Abraham. At the behest of Sarah, his wife, Abraham had sent Ishmael and his mother, Hagar, into the wilderness, but God had promised that he would make Ishmael the father of a great people. Local legend had it that Abraham had visited Ishmael in the wilderness and that together they had built the Kaaba in Mecca, the first temple to the one God in Arabia. This reminds us that our scriptures do not give the whole story. God's plans are bigger and more inclusive than ours.

This was music to Muhammad's ears, because it showed that the Arabs had not been left out of the divine plan, as they had feared, but were children of Abraham too. Hitherto, Muhammad had instructed his Muslim converts to pray facing the direction of Jerusalem. They were symbolically turning their backs on the pagan traditions of Mecca and reaching out to the God of the People of the Book. But in January 624, after ugly displays of sectarianism in Medina, Muhammad instructed Muslims to pray facing Mecca and the Kaaba built by Abraham. Instead of belonging to a sect or denomination, they must return to the faith of Abraham. Muslims must still respect the People of the

Book, of course, but it was idolatry to prefer a religious institution, a purely human system, to God himself.

Muhammad had made a declaration of independence. Muslims must break free of the narrow sectarianism that refuses to accept the faith of the stranger, the newcomer, or the foreigner. At various points in their history, Jews, Christians, and Muslims have all fallen pray to this temptation. But we can no longer indulge this idolatry. Our very survival as a species depends upon our returning to the spirit of Abraham, and going out to meet the other—not in a grudging spirit, but with the wholehearted joy, trust, and generosity that caused Abraham to fall on his face before the strangers at Mamre, recognizing that they enshrined the divine presence. *The Tent of Abraham* brings three religious traditions together so that we may all become more familiar with the faiths lived by the strangers around us.

INTRODUCTION

Hearing the Voices of the One Who Hearkens

THERE IS AN ABRAHAMIC FAMILY.

Like all families, it shares a story. But part of what it shares is that different members of the family tell different versions of the story. They are like people who have lived in the same house, gone to the same schools, traveled the same neighborhood—yet when you ask each family member to tell the family story, you might swear they come from different universes. So it has been for the different religions that trace their genealogical or spiritual lineage to Abraham.

Abraham had at least two wives; everyone agrees on that. Yet one branch of the family claims that he divorced one wife; the other branch, descended from her, fiercely denies it. Some remember that there was a third wife, or perhaps she was the second wife restored. (Let's see.... Maybe check with Cousin Esau; he's quite a curmudgeon, but he'll remember.) And everyone agrees there were at least two sons, born when Abraham was pretty old. Some say there were also several other children, born way way way late in life.

In some families, different experiences and different memories lead to rage, to bitterness and bloodshed. In other families, they lead to uproarious, juicy sessions of storytelling around the campfire, even laughter as the memories diverge and overlap.

Which way the differences are taken often depends on whether the different family members insist that they have it right, the others have it wrong. Or maybe they accept the differences as crucial to perspective. It takes two eyes, set a few inches apart, for human beings to see the world with depth and perspective. With one eye the world looks flat. With two eyes too far apart the separate visions cannot blend.

If you close your left eye and the right eye insists that the world it sees is the truth, the whole truth, and nothing but the truth, and then you close your right eye and the left eye insists its vision is the exclusive truth, then you're in trouble. You lose perspective, not only visually but also emotionally, intellectually, and spiritually. You may come to live in confusion, contradiction, despair.

The Abrahamic family has crystallized mainly into three religious communities—Judaism, Christianity, and Islam. Each of the three has had an enormous impact on the human race and on the planet. For much (not all) of their histories, their versions of the story have been contentious, bitter, violent. They have argued over variations on basic questions, like:

- Who was most entitled to inherit the land that Abraham walked?
- Which version of his relationship to God should guide the spiritual future of his family—should it be his "Godwrestle" when it came to justice for the city of Sodom, or his calm obedience of God's command to offer up his son?
- What about his wives: What should we make of their relationship to God and to each other and their children? Were they rivals or friends or both?
- Was this family holy or dysfunctional or both?

Ought the different family members to see each other as conflictual or complementary, horrible or honorable? So similar as to be competitive and frightening, or so similar as to be compassionate and friendly?

This book is intended to affirm and weave together the different strands of the Abrahamic stories, the threads of different colors, into a garment that can glow in beauty.

To do this, we bring together two strands of storytelling: the biblical version of the story and its later Jewish midrashic and Christian reinterpretations, and the Quranic version of the tale with the later Muslim hadith, the unfoldings of the meaning of the Quran. We treat them as multiple truths, two different eyes through which we can see with greater depth and perspective.

So you will find here not a single voice, a single program or platform, but multiple voices, telling the stories and interpreting them in multiple ways.

Academics and religious scholars have proposed that the mystical voice and the prophetic voice are different. The first is the voice of spiritual experience, they say, and the second that of work in the world. The truth is that at the time these stories were first told, there were no such artificial distinctions. Humanity was not separate from nature; there was no "theology" or "political science." There was no separation between cosmology, our place in the universe, and psychology, the way we view our inner universe.

In our design for this book, we have tried to reestablish this balance and harmony. Sometimes a story seems to call for action to establish a more just society, sometimes for introspection about how we treat the different voices within us, sometimes for both. We are hearing these stories not in the same way but in many different ways within a common uniting Reality, which the different traditions call by different names—Elohim, YHWH, Allah, Deus, God—but which, at least in all their Semitic versions, all mean Sacred Unity.

In our own time, it is more urgent than ever before to

try to bring this family and its stories into a fruitful relationship. Our planet is filled with dreadful weapons and with deeply dangerous practices like the addictive overuse of fossil fuels. In this world, religious quarrels can become immensely destructive.

Quarrels may begin over the differing meanings of God's will as it is reflected in our differing stories. Which member of the Abrahamic family more deeply exemplifies God's outlook on relationships between women and men? Which has better understood God's astonishing unfolding of modernity, bearing enormous new powers of the human race to reshape and endanger the world? Such quarrels may take on the great intensity that arises from matters of ultimate and existential consequence.

Quarrels may also begin not over the meaning of religious texts and of God's intention but over access to and control over land, water, oil, and military power, and still take on the intensity and commitment of religion when they are connected with religious identities, traditions, and practices. Struggles over the ability of one people who think we share a single story—"us"—to determine "our" own destiny, struggles over "our" honor and dignity, over "our" prosperity, become more threatening when religious teachings define who "we" are.

So the three of us who have shaped this book are sharing our sense of how these Abrahamic stories could be understood and used not to justify war and violence but instead to shape peaceable relations among our three communities.

There are three ways of drawing on the stories to grow the seeds of peace:

1. Simply coming together to listen to the spiritual journeys of our peoples—as well as the journeys of our individual selves—may deepen our understand-

ing and caring for each other. These stories could
be used around a metaphorical campfire for gatherings of Muslims, Jews, and Christians. The sharing
may help us see that the glimmering Unity all our
traditions affirm stands behind our teachings.

2. In all our communities, there are some people who
interpret our sacred texts in ways that stir rage
against the "other" and stir rage in the "other."
The way we are retelling these stories may instead
show people that there are ways to understand
them that more fully befit God's call for peace
and reconciliation.

3. Read anew, these stories point toward new possibilities in sermons, prayers, ceremonies, spiritual
practices, and social action.

This book is itself a journey through the histories, the
memories, and the imaginations of our three traditions and
communities. To chart the journey, we have organized the
book in the following way:

First, we present the two classic versions of Abraham's
journey: one as presented in the Torah and the Jewish midrash, which became the foundation for the story in Judaism
and Christianity, the other as presented in the Quran and
the Muslim hadith.

Next we offer three sections of essays that interpret the
story from each of our religious perspectives: as a Jew, a
Christian, and a Muslim living in the quandaries of our
own generation.

Finally, we present several documents that have
emerged from recent efforts to give living form to new understandings of the Abrahamic family. Among these are:

- a description of how Abrahamic conversations can
  be deliberately shaped to include not only the intellectual sharing of interfaith dialogue but also the

deep sharing of our prayer life and our different spiritual journeys, and how they can reach toward shared action to heal our wounded world;

• a poetic synthesis of the Jewish/Christian and the Muslim stories of Abraham that recognizes the family differences while making family connections and that could be used in all three communities as part of prayer, religious study, and dialogue;

• a call for peacemaking that addresses specific policy issues through the language of religious and spiritual wisdom;

• proposals for intertwining celebrations of the sacred seasons of the three traditions, and broadening the celebrations of any one of the traditions to affirm the others.

These documents all spring, in some way, from gatherings of a small group of people from the three Abrahamic traditions who have named themselves the "Tent of Abraham, Hagar, and Sarah."

As both the name of that group and the title of this book make clear, the tent of Abraham remains a powerful symbol. Ancient tradition teaches that Abraham, Hagar, and Sarah kept their tent open in all four directions of the world so that travelers who thirsted for water or hungered for food might be welcomed instantly and warmly, no matter the direction from which they came. Today we open this "tent of Abraham" to welcome all—Muslim, Christian, Jew, those of other traditions and communities or none—who thirst after Unity and hunger for peace.

JOAN CHITTISTER, OSB
MURSHID SAADI SHAKUR CHISHTI
RABBI ARTHUR WASKOW

TWO TELLINGS OF
ABRAHAM'S JOURNEY

ABRAHAM'S JOURNEY IN THE BIBLE AND THE JEWISH MIDRASH

Rabbi Arthur Waskow

THE EARLY CHAPTERS OF THE BOOK OF GENESIS PRESENT first a cosmic, then a mythic, and finally a macrohistorical setting for the intimate personal saga of Abraham and his family.

To understand the Bible's outlook on Abraham as a wanderer and seeker on the edges of empire, it is necessary to begin with the mythic tale of Genesis 11.

For Abraham—originally named Abram—is located in the line of Shem. Shem, one of Noah's sons, became a seed for change through the transformative event of the Flood. The seed then sprouted through another transformative event—this one the Bible's mythic "tower" story of the Sumerian/Babylonian Empire. The people of Bavel, or Babel—Sumerian Babylonia—had tried to make a "name" for themselves by mobilizing a single global language and building a great tower to reach heaven. But God shattered the project and the tower and cured their arrogance by shaping many new communities, each with its own name and language.

One of the bearers of a new tongue was Shem, whose very name meant "name." From "Shem" we derive the name of the local language tree we call "Semitic."

In the Torah's telling, God offered Shem's descendants —culminating in Abram—an utterly different way of making a name for themselves.

We should note that this biblical myth of the Tower of Babel had its roots in the ziggurats, the artificial mountains built by the Babylonians as temples to their gods. The Torah's account is a satirical critique of Babylonian culture. Although *Bab-El* in the Sumerian tongue meant "gateway of God," the Torah connected it with *balul*, the Hebrew word for "baffle" or "confound." The Torah rejoices in the shattering of the centralized globalism of one tongue in favor of grassroots communities.

Indeed, one way of seeing the Torah and its version of biblical Judaism is as a major response to Sumeria's imperial power, which was built upon the invention of monocrop irrigation agriculture. Faced with Sumeria's economic and military power, how were the Western Semitic tribes, who had been living as small farmers and shepherds in more decentralized polities, to respond?

The Torah sees this as a spiritual and religious crisis, in that any understanding of the Divine was profoundly connected with the path of human life in society. So any challenge to Sumerian culture included a challenge to the Sumerian gods.

Abraham became one of the heroes of the Western Semitic response to Sumerian power, pursuing and being pursued by a God who transcended the divinities both of Babylonia and of the Western Semites. For, as Abram, he grew up on the edges of the Babylonian empire, in a family that was moving toward its frontier but was still within its cultural frame. He broke out, geographically, culturally, and religiously. He traveled among the Western Semites but never became one of them.

Abram (whose name means "high father," or "father

magnified") was born in the tenth generation after Shem. He married Sarai ("queen"), whom he later said was his half-sister. She remained childless. His father, Terah, transported the family westward from Ur, a city in Upper Sumeria (now Iraq), toward Canaan but stopped part way in the town of Haran, very close to the present Syrian-Turkish border.

The Torah says practically nothing about Abram in Haran. But the midrash of the rabbis—commentaries that read the open spaces between the Torah's words and letters as if they were white fire, full of meaning as was the black fire of the letters and the verses—says a great deal.

Mostly they focus on Abram's spiritual searchings beyond the religious culture into which he was born. They describe his poking fun at the wooden statues of gods that his father helped to carve, and how indeed he destroyed some of them to show how powerless they were. And they describe how he came to acknowledge that beyond even the power of the sun and moon and stars there is a Unity that shapes them all.

Then this Unity, named YHWH, said to Abram that he must leave his land, his birthplace, and his father's house to "go forth toward yourself [*lech l'cha*]." The pun in the two words of Hebrew, which have the same consonant letters and differ only in unwritten vowels, can be only faintly hinted at in English: "outward bound/unbind inward." YHWH promised only a journey "to a land that I will let you see."

The name "YHWH" is usually translated as "Lord," but this is a later superimposition. There are several theories as to what the word originally meant. One is that the four letters are a conflation of those that make up the past, present, and future of the verb *to be*, and thus the name may mean "The Eternal." Another is that they are a causative form of the verb *to be* and thus mean "the One Who Brings

Being into Being," sometimes translated as "Holy One of Being." Still another theory focuses on how the letters sound if spoken with no vowels—*Yyyyyhhhhwwwwhhhh*—and heard simply as a breathing sound, thus "Breath of Life," or "Breathing Spirit of the World."

All these meanings reach toward the sense of a universal God, not limited to Israelite or Abrahamic cultures—and the third, the one that focuses on a breathing sound, does not even depend on Hebrew for its meaning. In all languages and cultures, people breathe. And not only human beings: all life forms breathe. Indeed, their breaths are interwoven: I breathe in what the trees breathe out; the trees breathe in what I breathe out. We breathe each other into life. God breathes us, we breathe God. That YHWH with whom Abram is in touch connects all life, all being.

Abram eventually reached Canaan, where YHWH let the Godself be seen by Abram. He built altars there to YHWH but was driven by a famine to visit Egypt, whose place-name in Hebrew is *Mitzrayyim*, which means "tight and narrow." It is doubly narrow in several ways, as the Hebrew suffix *ayyim*—used to form nouns of doubleness—hints, encoding in one word the English expressions "between the devil and the deep blue sea," "between a rock and a hard place."

From one perspective, the geographic Egypt was a long, narrow land, stretching a few miles wide and thousands long on both banks of the fertile Nile.

From another perspective, ancient Egypt cramped the body and the spirit into slavery.

And from still another perspective, this *"Mitzrayyim"* was a narrow birth canal, helping give birth to a prophet and a people.

Once in Egypt Abram feared the king would so intensely desire his extraordinarily beautiful wife Sarai that he would have Abram killed if he knew they were married.

So Abram and Sarai agreed to pass her off as his sister so that if the king took her for his harem, he would have no reason to harm Abram. But God revealed the truth to the king, who sent them away. They returned to Canaan.

Then Abram dealt with a series of quarrels over land and water—some with his nephew Lot, some with Canaanite kings. He made peace with Lot by offering him a choice of the most fertile land. He defeated the kings in battle but refused to despoil them.

Again and again, YHWH appeared to promise Abram the land for himself and his offspring. But Abram remained childless, and he finally challenged God to produce offspring or stop promising.

So God invoked an eerie ceremony. Abram fell into a trance, witnessed an uncanny fire offering of his herd animals, and once again was promised the land of Canaan for his offspring.

But still there was no offspring. So Sarai invited Abram to take an Egyptian maidservant, Hagar (whose name means "the foreigner," or "the stranger"), as a surrogate mother, to have a child who would be recognized as Abram's and Sarai's.

But when Hagar became pregnant, she began to preen herself. Sarai, fearing that she would be displaced, acted so nastily that Hagar fled into the wilderness. There, at a well-spring, she became the first person in the Bible to hear a *malach* of YHWH, God's messenger or angel, speak to her. The messenger pronounced a prophecy about her son.

The prophecy is usually translated this way:

Name your child Ishmael ["God hears"],
For God [*El*] will hear [*sh'ma*] his outcry.
He will be a wild-donkey of a man,
His hand against everyone,
Everyone's hand against him,
Yet then he shall dwell facing all his brothers.

From this translation—some version of which has been common in many languages for centuries—the prophecy seems hostile to Ishmael. However, the translation may be using "Ishmael" to encode the hostility to certain Arab communities—and later to Islam itself—that grew in some Jewish and Christian circles long after the Torah text was written.

For if we return to the Hebrew text, several of these words invite less hostile translations. For example, the word usually translated as "wild donkey" comes from a root that means "free-running." And for ancient Israel, the wild donkey was neither predatory, like a wolf or lion, nor docile, like a domesticated sheep or cow. It was free, not necessarily hostile or dangerous.

If we retranslate the ancient Hebrew, it might come out this way:

> Name your child "Ishmael," "God Hears,"
> For God will hear his outcry.
> He will be a free-running human,
> His hand in everyone's,
> Everyone's hand in his,
> And he shall dwell facing all his brothers.

God's messenger urged Hagar to return home and live under Sarai's power.

Following this encounter Hagar gave God a new name (the only person in the Hebrew Bible to do so): *El Ro'i* ["God of seeing me"/"God of my seeing"]. And the well was thenceforward called *Be'er Lachai Ro'i*, "Well of the Living One Who Sees Me."

As YHWH's messenger had spoken, Hagar did return to Abram's tent, she did bear a son, and Abram confirmed that his name would be Ishmael—"God Hears."

Then once again YHWH appeared to Abram. Finally the promise of offspring became a covenant. On God's side of this sacred agreement, YHWH said again that Abram's offspring would be greatly blessed, sojourners in all the land of Canaan. In addition, two new elements entered the relationship. YHWH gave Abram a new name: Abraham. God said that the new name meant "father of a multitude of nations," and that all the families of the earth would be blessed through Abraham. Sarai was renamed Sarah, both names changed by the addition of the Hebrew letter *hei*, a breathing sound (and the letter that appears twice in God's name).

And YHWH commanded the renamed Abraham to circumcise his own penis, through which a new child must be begotten, and to circumcise as well his son, Ishmael (now thirteen years old), all the men of his household, and, when a son was born to him, that son on the eighth day of his life. This eighth-day circumcision was to become a continuing practice, a sign of the covenant between God and Abraham, Sarah, and their descendants forever.

When Abraham, now ninety-nine years old, heard the promise of a child of his own body and that of Sarah, only ten years younger, he laughed—and implored God simply to give life and offspring to his son Ishmael. God promised that indeed Ishmael would be fruitful and from him would spring twelve mighty leaders, the number that made a great nation in the biblical world. But God repeated the promise that Abraham and Sarah would have their own son, and that he should be named precisely for his father's laughter: Isaac, or "laughing one."

Abraham did all the circumcisions that affirmed his side of the covenant, and God then fulfilled the long-standing promise of a child with Sarah.

Three travelers came to the open-sided tent of Abraham, Sarah, and Hagar. Abraham fed them, and then it turned out they were God's messengers, come to reaffirm the promise of a child. Again there was laughter—this time Sarah's, for she knew that she herself was no longer menstruating and her husband was no longer virile. So how could they have a child? Yet the visitors reaffirmed the promise.

The travelers went on their way toward the cities of Sodom and Gomorrah, where Abraham's nephew Lot had gone to live. YHWH took Abraham into a special confidence, warning him that the cities were about to be destroyed on account of their wickedness. But Abraham protested: "What if there were fifty righteous people in the city? Should they be swept away along with the wicked? What about forty-five? Forty? Thirty? Twenty? Ten? Should not the Judge of all the world do justice?" And God agreed to save the cities if there were but ten righteous people in them. So to ascertain the truth, God's traveling messengers went to Lot's house, the better to scout the situation.

Their visit itself precipitated the crisis. Sodom's law forbade hospitality to strangers. (According to later Jewish tradition, that was the real and radical sin of Sodom: hatred of foreigners, outsiders, strangers.) When Lot took the travelers under his protection, a lynch mob gathered outside his house. They demanded that he send out the travelers for them to rape. Lot, even more committed to the ethic of loving the stranger than to the ethic of loving his family, offered his daughters as substitutes. But the mob was not interested in sex; it was focused on humiliating the foreigners they hated.

They were already metaphorically blinded by their hatred. Through God's intervention they were blinded physically as well and were ultimately unable to harm Lot's household and guests.

So the messengers concluded that there were not ten decent people in the city. (Lot's family numbered only six.) They warned Lot that the city was about to be destroyed, and once he had fled, the city was consumed by fire that rained from heaven—as if a great volcano had erupted, or a nuclear bomb had fallen.

At last YHWH acted upon the covenant with Abraham and Sarah: she bore a son, whom they named Isaac, "laughing one." Now Sarah laughed again, in joy rather than derision, and welcomed the joyful, surprised laughter of the whole community.

But soon laughter entered from another quarter. Sarah saw Ishmael laughing in a way that distressed her—laughing at or with his younger half-brother.

Perhaps this laughter mocked and mimicked Isaac's laughing essence. Perhaps it was an admiring imitation, the older brother enjoying the younger's joyful music in the world.

No matter what Ishmael intended, his father's wife defined the situation as sibling rivalry. Here in the family of Abraham echoed the archetypal tale of sibling struggle— that of Cain and Abel (respectively, "possessor" and "mere puff of breath"). This one, though, was to end not in death but in reconciliation.

This pattern—struggle, anger, withdrawal by the first-born who has started out as the more powerful party, then ultimate reconciliation—arises again and again in the rest of the book of Genesis. Jacob and Esau, Rebekah and Leah, Joseph and his brothers, Peretz and Zerach, Ephraim and Manasseh—in each pair the tension rises and is resolved.

In this case, the conflict between the brothers replayed what had happened many years before, when Hagar fled into the wilderness while she was still pregnant with Ishmael. (The Torah often replays an important story with a new outlook, a new dimension. All the sibling stories might be seen this way.) Sarah demanded that Abraham send the maidservant and her son into the wilderness. Abraham demurred "for his son's sake" (perhaps a way of defusing concern that he might simply be lusting after Hagar)—but

God intervened to say that Abraham must hearken to Sarah's voice.

So Abraham rose early in the morning, provided Hagar and Ishmael a skin of water, and sent them out into the wilderness. But the water ran out. Faint and close to death, Hagar laid Ishmael on the earth beneath a bush. She walked away, refusing to see her child die before her eyes. She wept.

And God fulfilled the prophecy that decreed the naming of the boy: "*Yishma elohim* [God hearkened]," says the text, echoing the Hebrew form of the boy's name, *Yishmael*. God opened Hagar's eyes to see the well she had named the Well of the Living One Who Sees Me, all those years before. They drank—and survived for Ishmael to grow and prosper.

The Torah continues with the story of another dangerous passage for Abraham's other son, in which there are many parallels to the dangerous journey of Ishmael. But before that story is laid out, there is a brief detour. It is about Abraham's achieving secure access to a well. Why is it inserted before the parallel story of Isaac unfolds? Perhaps the Torah is hinting that the assurance of a well for Abraham depended on the assurance of a well for Ishmael and Hagar. Not till their lives and futures were secure could Abraham be safe.

And the method of achieving safety is in itself a lesson:

Abraham quarreled with a group of local shepherds about a well that he had been using to water his sheep. The shepherds dispossessed him. But he and the local ruler were able to swear the oath of a covenant, giving Abraham special access to the well in exchange for the goats and sheep that he presented to his covenant partner. They also set aside seven ewe lambs, making a physical symbol of a Hebrew pun: *sheva* can mean either "oath" or "seven." As they swore to keep the peace, the sight of the seven lambs gave vivid evidence of the oath. They named the well Be'er Sheva, the "Well of Seven/Oath."

After achieving the security of safe access to a well, Abraham entered on his riskiest adventure. God tested him, calling him to the second great journey of his life, once again saying, "*Lech l'cha*"—"go forth toward yourself." And here, "outward bound/unbind inward" culminates in an actual binding: Isaac's. Once again God commanded him to go toward an unknown destination that God would let him see when the time was ripe. But this time, Abraham was to take his son Isaac to this place that he would see, and there make an offering of him to God—an *olah*, a "going-up offering" that was conventionally done by burning the offering so that its smoke would rise to heaven.

Abraham responded only with "*Hineni* [Here I am]." As he had with Ishmael, he rose early in the morning to pack for the trip. Along with food and water, he took a knife, a fire-starting flint, and wood to ritually slaughter the offering and to begin its burning.

On the third day of the journey, Abraham lifted his eyes and saw from afar the place God had told him would be "the place of seeing/being seen." As they approached, Isaac called to him "*Avi*," ["Dad,"] and Abraham responded once again: "*Hineni*"—"Here I am, my son."

Isaac asked why there were all the tools for the offering but no lamb to offer. Abraham answered, "God will see to the lamb—my son." And, the Torah says, "the two of them walked on as one."

When they reached the mountaintop, Abraham laid out the wood for the offering and stretched Isaac out upon it, binding him to the sacred slaughter site, the altar. (This moment has for centuries given the whole story its name, the Binding, *Akedah*.)

Isaac seemed at this point to have surrendered his soul to God, accepting the fate he expected. Jewish tradition suggests that he asked to be bound so as not to flinch at the last moment.

Abraham lifted his knife.

Suddenly the voice of a messenger from YHWH, an angel (the Greek word *angelos* means simply "messenger"), called, "Abraham...Abraham!"

Some say the voice came twice because Abraham was so focused on the dreadful task he had accepted that he barely heard when his name first echoed on the mountaintop, and did not stop the descending knife. Only when the voice shouted in alarm did he hear and heed it.

On hearing the second outcry of his name, once more he muttered, "*Hineni.*" Then the voice said, "Do not lay a hand on the boy!"

"And now I know that you are in awe of God, for you have not withheld your son, this unique boy, from Me."

Abraham lifted up his eyes (like Hagar in the wilderness) and saw a ram caught in a thicket by its horns (as she had seen the well that saved two lives, the Well of Seeing). Abraham went and took the ram and raised its smoke to heaven, a burnt offering to God in place of his son.

As Hagar had named her well for "the Living One who sees," Abraham called this place "YHWH sees." Even in the days, long after, when the story was written down, the Torah says, one could still hear said about the place: "On YHWH's mountain is being seen." According to Jewish tradition, Mount Moriah, the "hill of seeing"—the center of the Temple and its offerings—was this same place.

Once the ram had been slaughtered and burnt as an offering, while Abraham was still upon the mountaintop, YHWH's messenger called yet again from heaven to renew the promise: because Abraham had offered his son, manifold blessings would grow into many seedlings from his roots, like the stars of the heavens and the sands of the seashore. All the nations of the world would follow at his heels and take blessing from his hearkening to God.

Just as the story of Ishmael's achieving safety through a well released the possibility for Abraham to find safety in peaceful access to a well of his own, so at the end of this fear-some journey, now that his other son was also safe , Abraham could return to his well, Be'er Sheva. And the Torah adds a note about the birth of a cousin to the family back in Haran—a daughter named Rebekah. The birth announcement offered one bare hint of possible comfort to the shaken Isaac or to the shaken hearer of his story: Rebekah was to become Isaac's wife, though he did not know it yet.

But the journey cannot be said to have a joyful ending. For Abraham returned to find that his wife, Sarah, had died. Some traditions maintain that on hearing where her husband had taken their son, she understood his intention and died in anguish.

In the life Abraham had shaped until this point, there remained but two important tasks: to mourn and bury Sarah, and to find a wife for Isaac. Yet it turned out there was more life yet to live.

The burial of Sarah and the carving out of space for his own grave beside her became a complex task. Until now, Abraham had been a "resident alien," wandering across a land that welcomed nomads, owning no land of his own. For a tomb, however, he decided to make a formal purchase. After intricate bargaining with the local owners, he bought a cave called Machpelah ("doubling"). There he buried Sarah.

And then he sent out a trusted servant to find a wife for Isaac. She must be from the family he left behind in Haran, but she must be willing (as Abram and Sarai had been) to leave her parents and journey into the unknown Canaan, to her unknown cousin Isaac.

And it happened that once again a well became central to the saga. The servant grew thirsty on his journey and paused at a well near the town of Abraham's brother. The first woman he met at the well had compassion on him and —even more important if she was to be a shepherd's wife in a nomad clan—on his camels, watering them first. It turned out that she was from Abraham's own clan, the Rebekah whose birth we have already heard announced.

Doubts vanished. There was no question that she was Isaac's destined wife. The negotiations between Abraham and Rebekah's brother Laban carried forward once again the unfolding of this family whose wellsprings poured out a future filled with blessing. Rebekah went forth with Abraham's servant on the journey to Canaan, lifted her eyes along the way to see Isaac walking in the fields, and was so deeply moved she fell from her camel to greet him.

Isaac brought her into Sarah's tent and at last was comforted for the loss of his mother.

We might think that at last Abraham's destiny was fulfilled, the next generation assured, and his own rest beckoning alongside Sarah at the double tomb. But no, there was one more spiral to the story. The old man married again—a wife named Keturah ("sweet-smelling spice").

According to the Jewish midrash, Keturah was Hagar. Over the years, Abraham had been visiting her in disguise, to make sure that she and her son were well cared for. At last they were reunited, and the last loose thread in his adventurous life neatly, sweetly tied. They had six children and even some grandchildren, whom he sent eastward to be the seeds of other communities.

At the age of 175, Abraham died. His sons—the Torah goes out of its way to call them, for the first time, "his sons" and to unite them instead of reporting their lives along separate pathways—came to bury him alongside Sarah, in the "double cave" of Machpelah. Then Isaac settled at the Well of the Living One Who Sees Me, the well that had saved Ishmael's and Hagar's lives. The Torah continues with the story of his children, twins who renewed the brothers' battle in even more intense and intimate ways than had their father and half-uncle.

Ishmael died at the age of 137. The Torah reports that he had twelve sons, the marker of a prosperous and powerful people (which would be repeated one generation later with Isaac's son Jacob). The last aspect of the prophecy that had shaped his life—the words YHWH's messenger had spoken while he was still in Hagar's womb—was fulfilled: no longer estranged from his brother Isaac, "facing all his brothers did he fall."

THE STORY IN ISLAM

MURSHID SAADI SHAKUR CHISHTI

THE STORIES ABOUT ABRAHAM AND HIS FAMILY UNFOLD IN A number of episodes scattered over many different chapters (called *suras*) in the Quran. These stories are mixed together with prayer, cosmology, exhortation, and practical advice for situations confronting Muhammad at the time. What confuses Westerners who first encounter the Quran is the lack of what they perceive as organization, or at least the same sort of organization one finds in the Bible: history, prophecy, wisdom literature, songs and psalms, gospels and epistles.

The Quran is not organized either by subject or chronology, even though it may be helpful for the beginning reader to understand it in these ways. The early suras of the Quran are revealed to Muhammad in Mecca, when the early Muslim community is still a minority, or counterculture. These suras are primarily cosmic hymns and wisdom literature, similar to those in the Bible. The later suras are revealed once the early Muslim community decamps under persecution and comes to live in Yathrib (later called Medina), where they are invited to set up their own ideal society. Then Muhammad is challenged to work out the practical ethic that the new community, like all spiritual organizations, needs. These later suras address particular situations and cultural conditions of the time, albeit from the standpoint of the highest guidance coming through Muhammad from Allah.

For Christians, this would be the same difference in language and context as that between the Beatitudes or Sermon on the Mount of Jesus and the Epistles of St. Paul. As a number of Christian theologians have pointed out, the former are universal wisdom; the latter address specific situations in the communities to which St. Paul writes. Both are "inspired," yet inspired for very different purposes. For a Jewish parallel, one could compare the language and context of Genesis, the Psalms, or other wisdom literature with that of the more specific communal rules for the early Hebrews mentioned in Leviticus or Deuteronomy (for instance, Deut. 22:11: "Thou shalt not wear a garment of divers sorts, as of woolen and linen together.")

Early Quranic commentators filled out the episodes in the Quran that concern Abraham and his family with sayings from other early Muslim authorities or from the Prophet Muhammad himself, the latter sayings called *hadith*. Different commentators told the stories in different ways, within the limits that the broad strokes of the Quran allow, and some trends in the ways they told the stories changed over time. The context for early Islamic understandings of the Abraham stories include pre-Islamic Arabian legends, stories told by Jews and Christians living in Arabia at the time of Muhammad, and interpretations by early Islamic commentators that sought to make sense of Muslims' place within the traditions of other "peoples of the Book," that is, various heterodox and orthodox strands of Judaism and Christianity.

The Quran does not mention Abraham's birth; however, Islamic legends accord him a miraculous birth, similar to the births of other prophets. His father, Terah, is the vizier of the Mesopotamian despot Nimrod, who is warned in a dream that the son of someone near him will be his undoing. Then Terah's wife, Anmuta, already well past menopause, suddenly becomes fertile again. Terah tries to stay away from her and goes to worship his idols, but he stays away a bit too long. Anmuta comes to find him and they make love on the temple floor, conceiving Abraham. Meanwhile Nimrod is looking everywhere for the threat to his throne and, like the biblical Herod, slaughters all male children that he can find. Anmuta hides the newborn Abraham in a cave, where he is raised by angels until he is four years old.

At this point, Abraham returns to his parents' home and, for the next forty years, challenges the idolatry of his family, the community, and Nimrod, escaping death in a series of miraculous episodes. The Quran relates several important turning points in young Abraham's life.

First, God shows the child-prophet "the heavens and earth," in a night vigil. He sees a star and mistakes it for God, but when it sets he says, "I don't like gods that set." Then the moon rises and the same thing happens: enchantment followed by disillusionment. Finally the sun begins to rise. "This must be it!" he thinks. But when the sun sets, he makes a new resolution: "I am done now with mistaking anything for the One Being. Instead, I turn my face towards the One who created both heaven and earth" (Quran 6.76ff).

Sometime after this, Abraham's clan asks him to stay home and guard their idols while the rest of the community goes to a festival. Instead, he destroys all but the largest of the idols, in the hands of which he places an ax. When his clanspeople return, they blame Abraham, but he pretends to pin the blame elsewhere: "The big idol did it! Ask the others!" he says. "You know they can't speak," his clansmen reply. "So why do you worship things that can't speak and can neither help nor harm you?" he retorts (Sura 21:51–67).

Finally, he confronts Nimrod himself (or is brought there by his incensed community). In an exchange similar to that between Moses and Pharaoh, Nimrod asks, "Who sent you?"

"The One who gives life and takes it away," replies Abraham.

"I do that also," says Nimrod.

After receiving God's permission, Abraham then takes four birds, cuts off their heads and has the rest of their bodies placed on four different mountaintops. Abraham calls the birds, and their heads reunite with their bodies, each one calling out, "There is no One but the One!" Abraham challenges Nimrod to do the same, but he cannot.

At one point, Nimrod throws Abraham into a furnace (like the Babylonian despot Nebuchadnezzar does to three young Hebrews in the Torah), and angels preserve him. These exchanges continue, escalating in scale, until Nimrod sends a whole army against Abraham. God sends an army of gnats in response. One of them crawls into Nimrod's brain and kills him.

It is at this point that Abraham leaves his home in Mesopotamia for the "Holy Land" (which the Quran calls at one point *al-ard al-muqaddasa*), an area roughly including present-day Syria, Lebanon, Jordan, and Israel. Either before he leaves, or on his way westward, Abraham marries Sarah. (The Quran and other Islamic literature do not relate the same Abram/Abraham and Sarai/Sarah name changes that the Torah does.)

The Torah tells of an encounter in which the Egyptian pharaoh tries to take Sarah from Abraham, and Quranic commentators (but not the Quran) repeat this story as an encounter with an unnamed tyrant or king living in Jordan. The events are largely the same. The tyrant wants Sarah.

Abraham says she is his sister, but this doesn't help. After the tyrant tries to take her by force, he is stricken with a seizure (or a withered hand, depending on the version of the story). The tyrant repents, Sarah prays for him, and he's healed. He then sends Abraham and Sarah on their way with Hagar, who is either his daughter or a servant (again, depending on the version). Ishmael is born, an event more implied than stated in the Quran itself.

After a brief stay at Beersheba (which is similar to the story in Genesis 21), Abraham, Sarah, and Hagar move elsewhere in Syria, where mysterious guests visit them. This episode parallels the story in Genesis 18, with some differences: Angels appear in the guise of men. Abraham brings them a roasted calf to eat, but they refuse to touch it. Because refusing hospitality is tantamount to an act of violence in a nomadic culture, Abraham and Sarah become very afraid of their guests. They are both already advanced in years. The messengers reassure them and say that they've come to give them news of a son (in one Quranic account, Isaac is named, and after him Jacob). According to the Quran, Sarah's reaction is either to laugh, as in the Bible, or to hit her forehead in agony, saying, "Me? An old woman!" Abraham then asks about their mission, and the angels relate that they are on their way to destroy the town where Lot lives. As in the Bible, Abraham pleads with the messengers for Lot's life. The angels reassure him that Lot's family (except his wife) will be spared (Quran 11:69–74 and 51:24–30).

The Quranic story next shifts the action from Syria to Mecca. While still in Syria, Sarah becomes jealous of Hagar, after the birth of Ishmael. It's unclear whether this is before the birth of Isaac or after (as in the biblical account). In any case, Abraham takes both Hagar and Ishmael (who in most accounts is still nursing) to Mecca, at the time a desolate place.

He leaves them under a tree, and as he begins to return, Hagar runs after him.

"To whom are you entrusting us?"

No answer.

"Is this God's will?"

"Yes."

Hagar is satisfied. According to Islamic tradition, Abraham then recites a prayer asking that Hagar and Ishmael remain safe and that others open their hearts and help them (Sura 14:37–38).

The water Hagar has brought with her runs out, and Ishmael becomes dehydrated. Hagar then runs between the hills of Safa and Marwa (near Mecca) seven times in distress, looking for help. (This "running" was part of the pre-Islamic pilgrimage ritual and became incorporated into Islam with this story.) Then she hears the voice of an angel, who scratches the ground near Ishmael with his heel. A spring of water bursts forth. This spring becomes the Well of Zamzam (meaning "abundant water"), a pre-Islamic sacred site, which is also important in the Islamic pilgrimage ritual. The angel tells Hagar not to worry, that her son and his father will build the House of God there.

A further Islamic legend says that a passing tribe, the Jurhum, sees a flock of birds circling and believes there must be water nearby. They find Hagar and Ishmael and ask permission to live at the well. The community grows, the Jurhum teach Ishmael to hunt, and he marries a local woman. Sometime thereafter Hagar dies. This legend ties the Abraham story to ancient Arab genealogical traditions, which considered the Jurhum linked to one of the original or "true" Arabic tribes, the Qahtan. According to this pre-Islamic tradition, the Jurhum originally controlled the sacred rites in Mecca and at the Kaaba, but eventually were driven from the city and died out before the time of Muhammad.

Many early commentators relate stories (again not in the Quran) that Abraham visited Ishmael in Mecca several times. The first time, Ishmael is out hunting. Abraham meets Ishmael's wife, who is rude and inhospitable. He leaves a (thinly) veiled message for Ishmael ("change your home's entryway"), which Ishmael correctly interprets as advice to divorce his wife and marry another. The second time his father visits, Ishmael is again out, but this time his new wife welcomes Abraham and offers him food and drink. A new coded message to Ishmael ("Good entryway!") affirms Abraham's blessing on his current domestic arrangements.

The third time Abraham visits Ishmael is the most important in Islamic tradition. Ishmael is actually home (trimming arrows). Abraham tells him that God has commanded him to build the Sacred House and that Ishmael is to help him. According to some Islamic traditions, a cloud or divine figure called the *sakina* (perhaps related to the Hebrew *shekhinah*, divine presence) shows them the exact spot. After they dig, they find the foundations of a much earlier shrine built by Adam after he and Eve were exiled from the Garden. According to this tradition, Adam was the first person to circumambulate the Kaaba. Abraham thereupon builds the Kaaba and Ishmael hands him (and/or looks for) stones.

At some point, Abraham needs a crucial stone for one of the corners and sends Ishmael to look for it. While he's away, the angel Gabriel arrives and gives Abraham the sacred Black Stone. According to Islamic tradition, the earlier Kaaba had been raised to heaven during the flood of Noah's era in order to preserve it, while the Black Stone was preserved in the middle of a nearby mountain. Abraham and Ishmael then recite a prayer from Sura 2:127: "O Sustainer, accept this from us, for you are the illumination of all seeing and all knowing." According to some Sufi traditions linked to this passage, Abraham used the sacred power of sound and breath to build the Kaaba, and the song that he placed into the Black Stone can still be heard.

These stories effectively tie the Quranic account with the biblical accounts before them, establishing a place for the new Muslim community as another tradition from the same source, with its own sacred book. At the same time, the pre-Islamic sacred sites and various pilgrimage rituals (both centered in Mecca and outside it) are reframed in a larger context that unites people across tribal lines as well as sends the message that there is only One Sacred Reality, shared by all.

The last part of the Quranic Abraham story opens with God telling Abraham to call all people for pilgrimage (Sura 22:27). Abraham responds that he doesn't understand how his voice can reach everyone. God tells him to call anyway, whereupon he stands near the Black Stone in the Kaaba, places his fingers in his ears, and calls in all directions (reminiscent of the Islamic call to prayer). Everyone on earth, as well as those not yet born, hears the call and responds, *"labbayka Allahumma labbayka!"* ("God, I am ready and at your service"), a phrase repeated throughout the Islamic pilgrimage ritual (and also known in a slightly different form from pre-Islamic rituals).

The Quran's brief references to Abraham's sacrifice of his son nowhere make clear whether Isaac or Ishmael was the intended sacrifice. Early Quranic commentators are divided on the subject.[1] Initial opinions in the first two hundred years of Islam seem to favor Isaac as the intended victim, perhaps because early Muslim commentators were making sense of the Quran and hadith by linking them more closely to related stories told by Christians and Jews. Later Islamic opinion shifts to favor Ishmael, and subsequent Islamic legends tie the sacrifice story into the pilgrimage ritual itself. In this version, Abraham and Ishmael build the Kaaba, and then Abraham calls the world to pilgrimage and performs the first pilgrimage himself. During the pilgrimage, God tells him to sacrifice his son, an act he attempts to perform at a traditional sacrifice site at Mina (near Mecca). God stops him and substitutes a sheep. Abraham then tells Ishmael to continue to live near the Kaaba and instruct people in the pilgrimage. A number of variations of the story exist in Islamic tradition, including one that has Abraham and Sarah both making the first pilgrimage and Isaac still as the intended sacrifice.

The Quran does not relate Abraham's death, but one story about it appears in Islamic legend. The Angel of Death appears to Abraham in a very handsome form.

"Who are you, looking so noble?" asks Abraham.

"The Angel of Death."

"Who could hate death when it comes in such a beautiful form?"

"Well," says Death, "this is the way I appear to prophets. Here's the way I appear to unbelievers." Death changes his appearance and Abraham almost faints.

"Okay! Return to your other form, please!" says Abraham.

Death is just about to take Abraham but can't bring himself to do it. So he returns later in the form of an old man and asks Abraham for something to eat. True to his traditional hospitality, Abraham loads a large tray with food and presents it to him. The old man begins to lift the pieces of food to his ears, eyes, and chest, as though he doesn't know what to do with it.

"I'm afraid I'm too old to eat," says the man.

"How old is that?"

"Two hundred years."

"I'm only six years from being that old," says Abraham, "and if that's what being two hundred is like, I don't want to live any longer!"

And at this point, the Angel of Death takes him. Islamic legend here repeats the biblical assertion that Abraham was buried in a field he had previously bought that also contained Sarah's tomb, a site in Hebron still sacred to Muslims, Christians, and Jews today.

NOTE

1. For a full examination of this subject, see Reuven Firestone's *Journeys in Holy Lands: The Evolution of the Abraham-Ishmael Legends in Islamic Exegesis* (Albany: SUNY Press, 1990).

PART I

JEWISH INTERPRETATIONS OF ABRAHAM'S JOURNEY

RABBI ARTHUR WASKOW

A Note on the Jewish Tales and Commentaries

FOR ABOUT THE FIRST FIVE CENTURIES OF THE COMMON Era, records were kept of the musings of thousands of rabbis who lived across a region several thousand miles broad—their parables and fantasies, their linguistic comments and legal rulings, their philosophical debates and thoughts on everyday life. These musings make up the Talmud.

One of the most important teachings of these rabbis was that the Torah was written not in black ink on white parchment but in black fire on white fire and that the white fire, the "blank" spaces, were waiting in every generation to be read anew.

In the blank spaces, the rabbis read and retold stories not written in the legible black fire. Stories of heroic effort and dangerous adventures, sorrow and despair. Teachings for later generations on how to live a life in touch with

God, in worlds utterly different from the world in which the black fire was encoded.

Midrash literally means "searching"—into the spaces between the letters, between the words, between the verses for the hidden treasures always to be found there.

And that is what the essays that make up this section seek to do, as they ask such questions as:

- What can we learn about the relationships of Israelis and Palestinians today from the dangers faced by Isaac and Ishmael?
- What did the two brothers say to each other when they met to bury their dangerous father, who had agreed to the banishment of one and narrowly avoided slaughtering the other?
- Did Hagar's tears water the wellspring that saved her life?
- In our own generation, has the ancient promise that Abraham's families would bless all the families of the earth become a grotesque caricature of itself?
- Abraham saw God; can we?

Some of these midrashic musings are focused on the way the stories of Abraham affect Jews when they are read on the two days of Rosh Hashanah. On these two days, the year and the souls of the faithful are renewed, and the Days of Awe begin their course, which climaxes on the twenty-six-hour-long fast day of Yom Kippur. During those ten days, every member of the Jewish community is called to ethical self-assessment, to repentance of wrongs done by the self, and to forgiveness of wrongs done to the self.

The ancient rabbis, thinking how to stir the community to take up this profound effort to turn themselves again toward God, chose as the public Torah readings for those days the story of the expulsion into the wilderness (and near death) of Hagar and Ishmael and the story of the binding (and near death) of Isaac.

So the stories take on a weight and seriousness even beyond the impact they usually have when they arise in the regular spiral of the weekly readings of the Torah. Understanding these stories in a new context by creating new midrash on them can, therefore, through the transformational depth of Rosh Hashanah, have an unusually powerful effect on thought, feeling, and action in the Jewish community.

And we might even think that precisely by lifting up these stories for us at this time of transformation, the sacred cycle of the calendar itself is asking us to transform the stories toward a healing of the broken family of Abraham—to transform them in the only way stories can be transformed: through midrash.

Welcome to midrash from our own generation. Welcome to some readings of the white fire.

WHEN ABRAHAM SEES GOD

I F WE ARE TO UNDERSTAND THE PROFOUND POWER THAT
Abraham bore when he addressed his family, his allies,
and his opponents in the countries where he sojourned, and
the trees and earth and wellsprings of the land itself, we
must begin with his way of seeing God.

Genesis 18 begins by saying, "YHWH made himself
seen [*va'yera*] [to Abraham] in [*b'*] the oaks of Mamre."

Since YHWH, the sacred unpronounceable name, has
no vowels and can only be "pronounced" by breathing it, I
translate it as "the Breath of Life."

Then the story continues: "... and he lifted up his eyes
and saw [*va'yar*] and here!—three men were standing upon
him, and he saw [*va'yar*] and ran... [to bring them near and
then to feed them]."

From this seeing Abraham brought the visitors to his
tent, and from this moment stems the teaching that the tent
was open in all four directions, to welcome passersby from
all the world.

Did Abraham, despite being allowed to see God, then
turn aside to feed these visitors?

I read this in a different way: first the oak trees themselves, and then the three visitors *were* the visible, see-able
presence of God. Usually we refuse to see God in each
other; but the Breath of Life on this occasion made the Divine Presence in these trees and in these people totally visible, see-able, to Abraham.

How can the Divine Breathing-Spirit of the world become visible in trees? Think about the rustling leaves, quivering as the wind rushes from them, in them, to them —quivering as the trees breathe out what we breathe in (the oxygen), and then breathe in what we breathe out (the carbon dioxide). This is the rhythm of life upon our planet. As we open our eyes to this rush of breath, we see God.

And it was not till Abraham saw God breathing in these oak trees that Abraham was able to see God in human beings.

Then he acted to affirm the holiness of what he now saw was utterly holy, by feeding God, who of course is never visible except in all that is around us—that is, is *always* visible if we open our eyes.

This way of seeing changes both how we act in the world and how we pray. Even now, many of us feel that in order to pray, to stand in God's presence, to see God, we have to turn away from each other, close our eyes.

But if we were to see as Abraham saw, if we never thought we are taking our eyes away from God when we look with care at trees or human beings or the rest of God's creation, if we were to look at the face of every hungry stranger and say, "O my GOD!" we would be expressing the "radical amazement" that Rabbi Abraham Joshua Heschel said God calls us toward, and we would stop separating the mundane from the holy.

And conversely, if we thought that indeed the only way to see God is to see fully the faces of the trees and of each other, then prayer and action would be integral, a profound difference from our usual divided attitudes and practices.

This is a way of seeing that can be learned. For example, in many synagogues, everyone faces east when the community chants the call to prayer, and so the congregants cannot see each others' faces.

But in some of our communities, we deliberately choose to stand in circles rather than in rows. The prayer leader reminds us to pause and look into each other's faces, one by one—pausing at each face to say, "This is the face of God. And this—so different, so unique. And this. And this."

And the leader may remind us to look with care at the "green faces of God," the trees and grasses, as well.

When we have done this enough times, we begin to believe it. It then becomes harder—not impossible, but harder—to forget that the faces we encounter every moment are God's faces. And to act accordingly.

This way of seeing seeded the future of Abraham's two families:

From it sprang the Well of the Living One Who Sees Me, which became visible to Hagar when she lifted her eyes from a moment of despair.

From it sprang the "Mount where YHWH sees and is seen," to which Abraham took Isaac for an offering and where he lifted up his eyes to see the ram that, becoming visible, saved Isaac's life.

This way of seeing is at the root of all the prophetic visioning that through millennia has marked the lives of all the families of Abraham.

THE CLOUDY MIRROR

THE RABBIS WHO TAUGHT JEWS ACROSS THE MILLENNIA how to celebrate the festivals highlighted as if in scarlet the intertwined stories of Ishmael and Isaac. Passages focusing on the most agonizing aspects of the longer saga—the all but lethal treatment of Abraham's two sons—are traditionally brought forward to be read on the two days of Rosh Hashanah, as Jews wrestle with their lives and seek both to repent the ill they have done others and to forgive the ill others have done them.

The two stories make us face the ill, as well as the good, that our forebears Abraham and Sarah have done to each other and to his sons. And the ill, as well as the good, that our Mother Sarah and our Tante (Aunt) Hagar have done to each other. And the good and ill that one of the boys has done to the other, or perhaps they have each done to the other.

Does Abraham repent? Do all the others? Do we? Do they forgive? Do we? Do they rejoice, laughing? Do we?

The Torah forces us to see the two stories as connected:

- In both, God tells Abraham to carry out the mission that puts the life of his son in deadly danger.
- In both, Abraham "rises early in the morning" to start the journey.

- In the one story, he lays a tree limb upon his son to begin the burning of the offering—while in the other, Hagar lays her son under a tree when he is at the point of death.
- In each story, only an act of God saves each son at the very last moment.
- In one story, Hagar lifts her eyes to see the well of Ishmael's salvation, which she has already named the Well of the Living One Who Sees Me; in the other, Abraham lifts his eyes to see the ram of Isaac's salvation, and Abraham names the place the "Mountain of YHWH's Seeing."
- In one story, Abraham's wife Hagar almost dies; in the other story, his wife Sarah does die as soon as the mission is accomplished.

And just as all these elements of the two stories double back on themselves, the very heart of these terrifying tales comes in the doubling of a crucial word: laughter.

The conception and birth of Isaac and his very name, *Yitzchak*, call out, "Laughter." And why does Sarah demand that Ishmael leave? The text says that she saw Ishmael was doing something strange to Isaac, her son: *mitzachek*. The word is from the very root that gives Yitzchak his name.

What does it mean? *Mitzachek* is usually translated as "making sport." The rabbis, clearly concerned over the seeming injustice of the expulsion, have cited the use of a similar word elsewhere in the Torah and argued that it means Ishmael was engaged in idolatry, or violence, or sexual license.

But the very fact that *mitzachek* is so closely connected to *Yitzchak* seems much more important. The similarity suggests that Isaac and Ishmael are very *similar* to each other. Not identical, but so similar that each is like a cloudy mirror to the other.

When we read this story on Rosh Hashanah in one Jewish community, we passed out several dozen small hand mirrors to the congregants. We asked them to look at themselves in the mirror, then puff a few breaths onto the mirror until it steamed up, then look to see their faces in the clouded mirror. Then as the mirror cleared, we asked them to look again, and to go through the process several times.

When we asked how this felt, the unanimous response was that it was crazy-making. Who am I? Am I clear, or blurred, or misshapen?

And so perhaps it was for Isaac and Ishmael—even more with another living being than with an inanimate mirror. Think of how children can drive grown-ups and each other crazy simply by imitating what others say and how their faces look.

So perhaps the constant presence of each son in the other's face was distorting both of them, making it hard for them to grow up together and yet grow into their own distinct identities.

So to become themselves, they must live separately, free of each other's control and imitation.

In this reading, Sarah is struggling for her son's identity. She feels he cannot grow up to be himself if he is constantly with this other, older, stronger self, so like but so unlike. So she separates him from that other cloudy "laugher."

The doubleness of laughter in the story is itself redoubled through the names of Ishmael and Hagar. Literally, the Hebrew *Yishma El* means "God will hear." The name is given first by God to the pregnant Hagar when God hears her sorrow over Sarah's harsh treatment of her. Then the name is confirmed in the desert when *God hears* the despairing cry of Ishmael and Hagar and offers them life and water.

But this name also has echoes in the other line of Abraham's seed. At the moment of the deepest despair and suffering of the Israelites in Egypt, the people cried out and their cry came up to God, *and God heard* their groaning and began the process of their deliverance from Egypt.

Again, so alike! The cry of despair rises from the exiles of the land, both sets of exiles, both seeds of Abraham: the cry rises from the child of Hagar and from the greatgrandchildren of Sarah. And the cry is heard.

The outcries echo each other; for the echo starts even before Ishmael is born, in the very name of his mother, Hagar. *Hagar* means "the sojourner," "the visitor," "the foreigner," "the stranger." When the Torah says that the Israelites were *gerim b'eretz Mitzrayyim*, "strangers in the Land of Egypt," that *gerim* is the same word as Hagar's name. And the connection is made even clearer because Hagar is called *Hagar ha'mitzria*, "Hagar the Egyptian"— the Egyptian stranger.

Over and over the Torah teaches us, "Love the stranger, for you were strangers in the Land of Egypt." Hagar the Egyptian was a stranger in our midst, we became strangers in her Egyptian land, and so we must learn to treat with love and equal justice the strangers in our land.

The story turns back upon itself, reminding us how like and unlike two peoples sprung from the same family can be.

Is this simply a story of the ancient past, bearing no echoes in our lives today? I think not. My thoughts come round to Palestinians and Jews: so like each other in so many ways, as Ishmael and Isaac were so much like each other!

- Palestinians and Jews dreaming of the same land.
- Palestinians and Jews yearning to govern themselves in Jerusalem.
- Palestinians crying out from refugee camps as Jews for centuries cried out from ghettos.

- Palestinians crying out now to be seen as a people of
  dignity, not pariahs, as Jews for centuries cried out to
  be seen as a people of dignity, not pariahs.

And—most poignant, perhaps most similar of all—
both peoples refusing to hear each other's outcry. For years,
the Palestinians said, "No Israel, so that Palestine can be
born." For years, the Israelis said, "No Palestine, so that Israel can be safe." Each people saying that the other's very
claim to love the land is illegitimate, for it undercuts their
own claim.

My mind goes back again to the banishment of Ishmael
in the Torah. So like, and so unlike! Is there no other way to
grow an identity but to banish what is both like and unlike,
thrust it out into the wilderness—almost to die? Ishmael
grew up to be an archer, his hand against everyone, everyone's hand against him. And Isaac grew up to be a holy victim—passive, a channel for the sparks of redemption rather
than himself a striker of sparks. His most important life
acts were to go with Abraham to be bound for sacrifice; to
accept as a wife the woman chosen for him; and to be so
blind as to be fooled by his son Jacob. Once the two brothers had separated, these two who had been alike become
most unlike. It is as if their father, the holy adventurer, had
been torn in two when his two sons split: one of them taking his holiness, the other his boldness.

No surprise that the split identities make war upon
each other: if you try to drive a part of your own identity
out by violence, send it out to die, it will come back to
threaten you, to kill you. Surely there must be another way
to grow your own identity?

Maybe not. It was the voice of God that confirmed
Sarah's desire, told the troubled Abraham to send Ishmael
away. The voice of God, the God of things as they must be.
Maybe there was no alternative to banishment; there might

have been no people of Israel at all and no Arab peoples either, if Ishmael had stayed with Isaac.

Maybe. But is there no path of possibility beyond the separation? Was there to be no moment in history when the two half-brothers would have grown their own identities so clearly that they could look past the cloudy mirror, see each other face to face? Is there to be no moment in history when the two peoples can see each other face to face? However one reads the first part of God's prophecy to Hagar about Ishmael, whether it portrays Ishmael as a wild and hostile bowman or as a nomad living free, it ends:

Facing all his brothers shall he dwell.

CALL ME ISHMAEL

THERE WAS A ROSH HASHANAH WHEN THE POSSIBILITY
that Isaac and Ishmael could live face to face entered inside my own face, my own heart, my own name.

On the first evening of that Rosh Hashanah, I had
chosen to highlight for the community the search for life-
giving water that pervades the entire month of holy festivals: Hagar's well and Abraham's, the yearning for rain
after six months of dryness in the land of Israel, a yearning
that grows through the harvest festival of Sukkot to urgent
prayers for rain at its conclusion.

I searched for a modern tale that might renew this
water-yearning, and recalled the first chapter of Melville's
Moby-Dick. There the teller of the tale describes how all the
people of Manhattan come thirstily to sit beside its rivers,
reaching for the seas beyond. I brought it to the evening service and read it aloud, from its beginning: "Call me Ishmael."

Overnight these words kept stirring in my dreams. I
had already been wrestling with the notion that the Rosh
Hashanah stories of Isaac and Ishmael could be read as
parables and teachings about the Israelis and the Palestinians. Not long before, I had written my younger brother
some thoughts about this parallel, this parable. To my astonishment, he wrote back a single sentence, entirely ignoring the political issues: "You realize of course that you are
Ishmael."

He meant that in our growing up, I had become the outsider, angry, holding myself apart and being held at bay by the rest of the family. He had been the good, placid, pleasant son. His note was the first hint of an emerging anger on his part, and from it we began uneasily exploring the distances between us.

Call me Ishmael.

And then, the next morning, I was invited to come up to say the blessings over a portion of the Torah reading. The custom is to call out the Hebrew name of the person who comes up. When someone came to ask for my name, my mind fell into a tumult. I would normally have said the name I had been given on the eighth day of my life, in memory of a grandfather who had died long before I was born: "*Avraham Yitzchak*, Abraham Isaac."

Suddenly—there was ringing in my ears and heart— I heard the words I had read the night before: "Call me Ishmael."

And the sentence from my brother: "You are Ishmael."

In the tumult, I found myself completing the unspoken triangle of my name, telling my fellow congregant, "My name is *Avraham Yitzchak Yishmael*"—Abraham Isaac Ishmael.

He looked at me askance, seeing my uncertain face: "Are you sure? I tell you what; I'll come back in a couple of minutes to ask you again, when it's the actual moment to call you up to Torah."

I trembled. When he came back, I said the name with more assurance. He shrugged and called it out, as is the custom. I rose—and another congregant looked up laughing, his face lit up with the joke. "That's not your name!" he said.

I turned red with fury: how dare he make a mockery of my serious life's turning?

And then I paused: it was like replaying the story. I laughed too.

"Like Sarah!" I thought. As she had laughed at the ridiculous notion of her giving birth, so I had to laugh and admit that changing my name really was funny. What a theatrical gesture! How ridiculous! And then, when someone else had dared to laugh at me, suddenly I could see nothing funny in the laughter. So also Sarah...when Ishmael dared to laugh.

I said the blessings, then turned to hear the Torah portion. I had been so involved in deciding whether to rename myself that I had no idea where we were in the text. So it was a great shock in that moment to hear sentences about Sarah's laughter and the birth of Isaac. *Yishma El,* "God heard"—and the Torah had spoken straight back to me. I had chosen right, my name had been confirmed.

And not with a reading about Ishmael—that would have been obvious and static. My choice had opened up the next birth, too. By making true and audible the Ishmael part of me, perhaps I had begun the process of giving birth to Isaac. Maybe now I could allow the Isaac part of me to come to life—the laughing one whose laughter is not a mockery but joyful: the holy one.

Abraham Isaac Ishmael. As if the sound waves of new life, beginning at the end of my name, were moving back through it. Maybe, maybe, maybe,...back toward the source, toward Abraham, toward the holy adventurer, toward wholeness.

Indeed, for me, the story only began with that renaming. Becoming this conscious fusion of the love/hate triangle in the story forced me into places I would not have named. Whenever there was a murder, a massacre, by either the children of Ishmael on one side or the children of Isaac on the other, I felt my own guts, my own soul, torn apart. When there were moments of peacemaking, I felt whole.

Perhaps, I thought, every Jewish man should add "Ishmael" to his name, and every Jewish woman, "Hagar"? And every Palestinian, or even every Muslim, should add "Is'haq" or "Sara"?

How much of every one of us is Ishmael or Hagar, cast out into the desert?! How much of us is Isaac, seeing only the knife above our head, gone quiet, meditative, our eyes turned inward, uncertain of the visible world around us?!

The third corner of the triangle, the name that got left out when I was born, the name that got written in invisible ink, the name that got called out in a cry of silence, was also me. Left out.

So I have had to live through what it meant to love being Jewish but stand one step outside the door. I learned how my concern for Ishmael the Arab made me Ishmael the outcast in many Jewish eyes. And I learned how deeply Jewish it is to be the outsider, even the Jews' own outsider. I learned how deeply Jewish Ishmael was. It was as if the more I learned about being the outcast Ishmael, the more I understood about being the holy nebbish Isaac—and how being holy made even Isaac into an outsider in the world.

IN GAZA, WHERE WAS
ISAAC'S ANGEL?

IN 1967, TO EXPLAIN WHY HE WAS SPEAKING OUT AGAINST the Vietnam War, Rabbi Abraham Joshua Heschel told the story of a young Polish Hasidic boy who cried when he read the story of Abraham's near-sacrifice of his son Isaac.

"Why are you crying?" said his teacher; "You know that the angel saved Isaac's life."

"But what if the angel had come a moment too late?" said the boy.

Said Heschel in 1967: "Angels are never late. But sometimes human beings are."

On the first day of Rosh Hashanah in 2000, in the Jewish year 5761, we—all of us—were too late.

In Gaza on that day, a twelve-year-old Palestinian boy was shot and killed in a cross fire of bullets between Israeli soldiers and Palestinians. So was the ambulance driver who tried to rescue him, as the boy's father begged them to stop shooting.

By the second day of Rosh Hashanah that year, almost all Jews had read in the Torah:

And Abraham stretched out his hand.
He took the knife to slay his son.
But YHWH's angel/messenger called to him from heaven
    and said—

45

"Abraham, Abraham!!"
He said: "Here I am."
He said: "Do not stretch out your hand against the lad,
    do not do anything to him!"

But that year, on the second day of Rosh Hashanah, we read in our newspapers a different version of the story. William Orme wrote, in the *New York Times* of October 1, 2000:

> [The twelve-year-old boy Mohammed Aldura] was filmed by a foreign television crew as he cowered behind a cement block with his father, who shouted at the Israeli soldiers to hold their fire. The ambulance driver was killed as he tried to rescue the boy. The excruciating scene, including the boy's screams as he was hit by the fatal gunfire and the father's cries of horror, was broadcast on Israeli and Palestinian television tonight.

And the Associated Press added:

> The boy screamed in panic as shots hit a wall just inches over their heads. Seconds later, [he] was fatally struck in the abdomen. He loosened his grip on his father and slumped over.
>
> Seriously wounded, the father, Jamal, shook with convulsions, rolled his eyes skyward and lost consciousness. He was hospitalized in Gaza and was expected to recover, family members said Saturday.
>
> An ambulance driver was killed trying to rescue them...

In the months afterward, some Israelis asserted that the bullets that killed Mohammed very possibly came from Palestinian guns in the melee. I cannot see that this makes very much difference. It was the situation that killed him, the readiness on all sides for bloodshed. And the lesson is the same.

So this is what Rosh Hashanah has come to?—the reverse of the Torah's story of the binding of Isaac. For here the father tries to protect the child, while the messengers of God—ourselves—do not speak out to save him.

More than five years later, thousands have died—some Israelis, some Palestinians, some from other countries—in the bloodshed that began that day.

Did Mohammed have to die because the Jewish people must insist on political sovereignty over that very rock where Isaac was bound and where the angel saved him?

Did Mohammed have to die because the Palestinian people were ready to use violence to assert its own control over the very rock where the first Mohammed rose to heaven, flying on the wings of the One God, who has, according to the Quran, made nations and communities diverse so that we could learn from and love each other, not so that we could hate and kill each other?

We had barely begun the ten days of *tshuvah*, "turning" or repentance, and already as a people had to face our share of responsibility for the death of this young Isaac (only, of course, he was a young Ishmael, Abraham's other son) and of other Palestinians—and the responsibility we share for the deaths of Israelis as well, who are still sent to die in order to occupy the territory that must be the grounding of a Palestinian state if there is ever to be peace.

What are the most authentic and effective ways to speak in defense of Jewish values and in defense of the Isaacs and Ishmaels who may well keep on dying?

First, we need to speak to our own deepest selves. Jews who have any serious spiritual commitments must ask themselves whether it is a religious obligation or an act of idolatry to make physical possession of the rock on which

Isaac (according to the story) was almost sacrificed such a central element of Judaism that we are prepared to die and to kill for it.

The Torah story seems to teach that indeed we do feel the call of a voice telling us to kill for some vision of a value but must not act upon that voice. Instead, we must attune ourselves to hear the deeper teaching of a deeper voice. Indeed, for centuries Jews have learned to honor both the faithfulness of Abraham to follow God's command, and the compassion of a God who forbade the killing of this child, and of all children.

Is not the story itself, the Torah that teaches us, our crucial possession—more important than this physical rock where long ago we stopped offering our children and our animals, in favor of offering our hearts to the Rock of Ages?

Is it not we ourselves, and only we ourselves, who can take this "rock of ages" from ourselves—by turning this hill into an idol?

Possession of (part of) "the land" is one thing. On it human beings can live, make a living, grow a culture, govern themselves.

But possession of a rock?

Killing and dying to keep it?

Is it not our religious task to take action and to educate against this idolatry?

It is also my opinion that Muslims bear a religious obligation to teach that killing to control the beauty of the dome above the rock betrays the meaning of the dome and of the rock. A nonviolent resistance to oppressive intervention is at its root utterly different from a violent one.

But whether Muslims undertake this teaching or not, the Jewish obligation does not waver.

Secondly, how do we speak to the official American Jewish leadership, many of whom criticize proposals for even limited compromises for sharing sovereignty over the Temple Mount?

How do we speak to any Israeli government, remembering that even a peace-oriented government in the year 2000 did not prevent and did not condemn Sharon's arrogant visit to the Haram Al Sharif/Har haBayit, but instead supplied him with an amazing entourage of some twelve thousand armed men to assert Israeli control; which did not order soldiers to restrict themselves to tear gas in addressing rock-throwing protests by outraged Palestinians but allowed the use of lethal weapons instead; and which then continued for years to fuel a growing rage among Palestinians.

For even while the Oslo peace negotiations continued, the Israeli army was still demolishing Palestinian houses, driving roads through Palestinian lands in ways that isolated different sections of the emerging Palestine from each other, and allowing more settlers to arrive on the West Bank.

How do we speak to the Palestinian Authority, calling on them to pursue their most decent vision of themselves through vigorous nonviolent action? To act with vigor to oppose and punish terror? For it is also our responsibility to say to the Palestinians that precisely because we understand their rage, we believe they must express it in nonviolent ways if their rage and Israeli fear are ever to be resolved in a decent peace.

And then how do we speak again to Israelis, urging them also to work out nonviolent responses to murderous terrorism—responses to transform, not merely traumatize, the Palestinian society that tolerates terrorism?

How do we speak to the American government, saying that Jews do not support a mindless idolatry regarding possession of that rock—do not support the smashing of Palestinian homes and the cementing of Palestinian farmland?

As we move from Rosh Hashanah to Yom Kippur, we remember that Yom Kippur is intended to be a day for confirming our commitment to choose life. As the Prophet Isaiah said in a passage that we read on Yom Kippur itself, fasting alone is not the point. The point is to act on behalf of the poor, the oppressed, the imprisoned.

And perhaps there is a deeper meaning still to this story that we not only read but live. Many readers today see the story of the binding of Isaac as the story of a "paradigm shift" in the religious life of Canaan, thirty-five hundred years ago. Perhaps the surrounding culture had believed the sacrifice of firstborns was a necessary, profoundly religious obligation for the sake of a fruitful future, filled with children. Perhaps it was at this moment, or through this story, that the family that gave rise to Israelite culture became convinced that child sacrifice is forbidden, not required, and began to offer animals instead.

No doubt this shift took not a moment, but an agonizing struggle over years.

Today, from the death of Mohammed Aldura and from all the other dead, perhaps we must learn a new paradigm shift in our religious lives.

Till now, Judaism and Islam have each insisted that one people alone had a sacred relationship to this land where Abraham, Hagar, and Sarah walked, where Ishmael and Isaac were born.

Now God calls out to us for another paradigm shift:

Each of the families of Abraham, at this moment in our history and the history of the planet, must affirm that both of us have a sacred relationship to the land.

So each of us must—not reluctantly and grudgingly, but with joy and celebration—welcome the other as well into a peaceful sojourn in the land, each of us determining our own lives, within a context of honoring each other's choices.

Why does God call out to us at this moment? Because we have the opportunity to model together what all the na-

tions of the world must do. In this generation when all nations must learn to share the great unboundaried earth or
in our failure shatter life upon this planet, our two peoples
can model how to share a single land.

For we ourselves must become the messengers of the
Most High, calling out to ourselves and to each other and
to all nations:

Do not stretch out your hands against our children!

THE TOMB AND THE WELL

T HE STORY OF ABRAHAM'S DEATH ASCRIBES POWER TO TWO places, a tomb and a well:

> Now these are the days and the years of Abraham, which
> he lived:
> A hundred years and seventy years and five years, then he
> expired.
> Isaac and Ishmael his sons buried him in the cave of
> Makhpelah
> In the field that Abraham had acquired.
> There were buried Abraham and Sarah his wife.
> Now it was after Abraham's death that God blessed Isaac
> his son.
> And Isaac sat by the Well of the Living One Who Sees Me.
> (Gen. 25:7–8a, 9–11)

The tomb is "acquired"; at the well, one "sits" and "is seen." Let us explore the meanings of these two places, these two life paths.

Almost the entire story of this tomb is about its acquisition. When Sarah died, Abraham bargained with Ephron the Hittite precisely so that he would acquire the Cave of Machpelah, lest it come to him purely as a gift. From Genesis 23:3 to 23:18, we hear about the dickering; then in one

verse we learn that Abraham buried Sarah there, and in two
verses (Gen. 25:9–10) we learn that Isaac and Ishmael buried Abraham there.

In modern times, this acquisition has been cited as a
model and prototype for Jewish ownership of the entire
land of Israel.

But on deeper reflection, this understanding is perplex-
ing. Abraham began his bargaining by making clear that he
is a *ger v'toshav imakhem*, a "sojourner-settler with you." He
is not normally entitled to own land as a permanent holding
for generations to come. He needs a special dispensation in
order to acquire this property.

This is exactly the same formula with which YHWH
explained in Leviticus 25:23 that the land must not be sold
beyond reclaim, for the Israelites are *gerim v'toshavim...
imadi*—"sojourners-settlers with Me."

So Abraham was the model sojourner-settler, and his
offspring were to learn that in this very land they were not
to be owners but sojourners-settlers. Yet he acquired this
particular piece of land, beyond reclaim. He did with this
piece of land exactly what the God of Torah says must not
be done—and yet the Torah approves his acquisition.

How come? What is this "acquisition" for?

A grave. As if only the dead can "own" land; the living
simply sojourn on God's land.

Owning rigidifies what had been fluid. Death rigidifies
what had been fluid.

Now let us turn to the other aspect of the story. Isaac and
Ishmael survived their dangerous father. Isaac went to live
at the Well of the Living One Who Sees Me.

Where did this well come from? It was the flowing well
through which "God hearkened" and saved his brother Ishmael's life, turning his name into a reality.

Hagar was the first of the biblical figures to be connected with a well. This one, first revealed to her when she was pregnant with Ishmael and feeling badly treated, was shown to her again just as Ishmael seemed at the point of death.

She had cast her son beneath a bush—a tiny oasis whose roots must have gone deep to find a source of water. She hoped the bush would keep the sun from scorching him. (The "casting" is from *tashlich*, the word that means not throwing trash away but, like Jonah when God cast him into the sea, being placed where the future can be transformed.)

Hagar closed her eyes, for she was unwilling to see her son die.

She cried, and her eyes poured tears into the earth.

And then God opened her eyes and she saw a well with water that she gave to Ishmael.

Surely this was once again the Well of the Living One Who Sees Me, which she had first seen years before when her own body could give Ishmael his nourishment.

And surely it was her tears themselves, falling into the earth, that gave rise to this wellspring.

Perhaps Hagar closed her eyes not in resignation but in a direct challenge:

Refusing to see her son so as to force God to see him— to open the "well of seeing" that she had seen so many years before. And so God does.

Refusing to hear her son so as to force God to hear him as she had been promised long ago.

And indeed God heard and saved their lives, watering their future as Hagar's eyes had watered the earth and God's own self: *Yishma elohim!* God heard! "Yishma'el" becomes his name in fact as well as in truth.

It is there, at the Well of the Living One Who Sees Me, that after they come together to mourn the father who had endangered both his sons, the son of Hagar ("the stranger") can live at last with the son of Sarah ("the queen").

And what does Isaac do? *"Vayeshev,"* he sat there (Gen. 25:11). He did not need to wander, he did not need to own. Like a practitioner of Zen, he sat.

He let YHWH see him.

If we the living give up our attachment to the rigidity of acquiring, we can sit calmly to drink at the flowing wells of vision.

The burial of Abraham where Sarah was buried causes us to recall the story of Sarah's death. She died just after the naming of another sacred place of seeing: Abraham names the mountain where he bound Isaac for sacrifice "YHWH Sees." According to Jewish tradition, though it is not specified in the Hebrew Bible, this hill long afterward became the place where the Temple was built and burned, rebuilt and burned again.

And today it is one of those sacred places whose "ownership" has swallowed many deaths.

Many years ago, the Jewish sages decreed that this place was not one we are supposed to physically inhabit, but a place we are supposed to physically avoid. We taught ourselves that our most sacred place is one we do not "own" and cannot even set foot on.

Why? Because we might inadvertently step into that space where once there was the Holy of Holies, the deepest inner aspect of the Temple. Why not do this? Because the Holy of Holies itself was a place to be entered only by one person for one moment every year: the high priest, at noon on Yom Kippur.

Our non-ownership was holy. This was a radical critique of idolatry. It teaches about space—don't try to own it!—what Shabbat teaches about time.

This wisdom of not owning and of staying off the Temple Mount in effect expanded the Holy of Holies, defining the entire Temple Mount as the Holy of Holies and *Mashiach*, the Messiah, as the one "high priest" who could someday enter it.

Of course we cannot do without land altogether. We are physical creatures who at our healthiest must have a land to "sit" in, a well to drink from, a brother or sister to see us. How can this be done without "acquiring" the land?

By sojourning and sitting, like Father Abraham and Tante Hagar, and like Isaac when God came at last to bless him.

How do we "sit"? By treating the land with loving respect, living not on its back but beside its well of life, encouraging its flow instead of draining its wetlands, or pouring poison into its rivers, or (like modern Israeli settlers on the West Bank) using scarce water for swimming pools instead of letting it flow to Tante Hagar's kitchen.

For exile, alienation, estrangement, cannot be solved by acquiring, possessing, owning—by rigidity. It can only be eased by acknowledging that possessiveness is itself a form of exile. By letting the water trickle through our fingers.

And by letting the water trickle through our eyes. Through grief.

The grief of two brothers at their father's grave is connected with the grief that Hagar and Ishmael had felt so many years and tears before. There was a reason that Isaac moved directly from his father's grave to the well where tears had given life.

The tears had come from Hagar's opening her eyes to see the truth, and the open eyes came straight from God.

Indeed, the well of seeing stood alongside a mount of seeing, where grief had also been poured forth.

For when Abraham took an even more direct hand in threatening the life of his other son, Isaac; when at the last moment Abraham heard a messenger from God commanding him to let the boy live; when according to the rabbinic midrash Isaac had already been blinded by the tears of the angels pouring into his eyes—Abraham too lifted his eyes, he too saw.

Just as Hagar had named the well for seeing, Abraham named the mountain "YHWH sees" and it became known as the "mountain of YHWH seeing" (Gen. 21).

These stories of Isaac and Ishmael are obviously intertwined and echo each other. In our generation, some have suggested that this echo is meant to convey that God's test of Abraham in regard to Isaac emerges from Abraham's behavior toward Ishmael. He expressed concern, but not conviction, when the moment came to spare Ishmael his ordeal. And so he himself had to create the ordeal for his other son. Not just the stories but the fates of the two sons are intertwined.

The fullness of the prophecy that Ishmael will ultimately live facing all his brothers was not lived out until after Abraham, the father who would have allowed both sons to die from his own actions, had himself died.

That was when Abraham's sons Isaac and Ishmael came together to bury him (Gen. 25:9–11). Indeed, only in this passage are they named together as "Abraham's sons," as if to teach us that they became truly his sons—and joined together—only by joining in their grief (or relief? or both?).

Only after that are they able to live face to face with each other; only then does the prophecy come true in which Ishmael is to live "facing all his brothers" (Gen. 25:18).

The two are able to live together only after they have mourned the most dangerous and threatening person in their lives.

Now—what does this weave of text and midrash have to say about today, about grief, about mourning, about the lethal violence within the family of Abraham in our own generation?

In the last century, both peoples have experienced disastrous abuses—the Shoah ("destruction"), the Naqba ("disaster"). Though the Shoah disaster was far more lethal, each left deep wounds and scars, yet unresolved, on the soul of each people.

And so we see that two abused peoples, still suffering, are thrown into conflict with each other. For each, an act that in its own eyes seems defensive is seen by the other as abusive.

Each grieves its own dead, killed at the other's hands.

We might draw a lesson from the shared grief of Isaac and Ishmael, and the release it gave them to face each other. Can Jews and Palestinians together share feelings of grief about the deaths that members of our two peoples have inflicted on each other?

Indeed, there has arisen a prophetic and pioneering group of Palestinians and Israelis who *together* mourn the deaths of their children, their sisters and brothers, their parents—killed by someone from the other side.

They mourn together and they work for peace, against the hatred that consumes those among either people who mourn only the deaths in their own family and turn their grief into rage.

So Jewish and Arab or Muslim groups might, ideally, come together to express publicly their grief at all these deaths. Where joint ceremonies cannot be arranged, let them do this separately.

And where even this cannot be arranged, where one community or congregation will not agree to mourn the dead of another, let those who will mourn the dead of the other go ahead and do so.

Among Jews, one appropriate and important time might be on Yom Kippur, after the ten days in which we are to do *tshuvah*—turn our lives in more just, peaceful, and holy directions.

The traditional Torah reading on Yom Kippur morning

includes a passage in which the high priest sends one goat out into the wilderness (like Ishmael in the story we traditionally read on Rosh Hashanah), and sacrifices another—on the same mountain where according to tradition, in the other Rosh Hashanah story, Isaac was bound for sacrifice.

These two goats echo Isaac and Ishmael. The goats can be seen as our Yom Kippur act of *tshuvah*—no, we will not do this to human beings, only to goats. And then we stop doing it to goats as well; we only tell the story.

And now on Yom Kippur, we could take one more step toward *tshuvah*. To the reading about the goats, we could add—or even substitute—as a Torah reading the passage about Abraham's death. (For synagogues where this seems *halakhically* or liturgically difficult, the passage could be read as "study," not from the Torah scroll.)

And immediately after reading it, the congregation could read the names of both Palestinians *and* Jews, both Iraqis *and* Americans, who have been killed in the conflicts of the past years.

Then there could be congregational discussion in a Torah-study atmosphere about how this passage bears on the Israeli-Palestinian conflict.

This reading could be followed by either the full mourners' Kaddish or just the last paragraph of the mourners' Kaddish (to distinguish this from the Kaddish said in memory of those who are closest and most beloved).

In the *oseh shalom* paragraph, after *v'al kol Yisrael*, the phrase *v'al kol Yishmael v'al kol yoshvei tayvel* could be added: "May there be peace/harmony for all Israel and all Ishmael and all who dwell on the planet"—that is, for the Jewish people, and for the Palestinian and all Arab and Muslim peoples, and for all endangered human cultures and all endangered species on the earth.

When either community mourns the deaths only of those on "its side" who have been killed by those on "the other side," the outcome is often more rage, more hatred, and more death. If we can share the grief for those dead on both "sides," we are more likely to see each other as human beings and move toward ending the violence.

BANISHMENT AND OFFERING:
THE GOATS OF YOM KIPPUR

W E READ THE STORIES OF ISHMAEL'S BANISHMENT AND
Isaac's binding on the first and second days of Rosh
Hashanah. Ten days later, we observe Yom Kippur.

These ten days are the days of *tshuvah*, of turning:
Turning ourselves in a new and more holy direction. As-
sessing the ways in which, like clumsy archers, we have
aimed at the bull's-eye but missed the mark. Turning our
selves and our life paths more closely toward the truth,
clearing up our relationships with others, making restitu-
tion for the wrongs we have done them, seeking their forgiveness and forgiving those who have harmed us. And
then, only then, seeking and finding forgiveness from God,
from the intertwining wholeness that unifies the universe.

Is there a path from our reading the troubling tales of
Rosh Hashanah to finding forgiveness on Yom Kippur?

The banishment of Ishmael and the binding of Isaac
are the two acts of Father Abraham's that we might think
most call for *tshuvah*. Is the message, echoing down the millennia we Jews have read these passages on these days, that
we must somehow, someday, do *tshuvah* for these two
actions?

Perhaps we need not condemn them in Abraham. He
was acting on God's orders, and both stories end with
God's intervening to save the life that he and Abraham had

jeopardized. Perhaps we should read the stories themselves as tales of God's own *tshuvah*.

But what about ourselves? Must we turn ourselves to some other way of acting? And not just turn ourselves, but thereby help God turn, help "necessity" turn, help the bedrock of the universe turn in a new direction?

What story do we read on Yom Kippur? We read a description of how our people celebrated Yom Kippur in the days of the traveling "shrine of the presence" in the wilderness, and then in the Holy Temple when it was settled in Jerusalem.

According to the story, we placed our sins upon the head of a goat that was chosen by lot and sent that goat out to wander in the desert with our own sins upon its head. And at the Temple, the very place where, according to tradition, Abraham bound Isaac as an offering, we sacrificed another goat—also chosen by lot.

One goat, you might say, for Isaac, and one for Ishmael. It is as if the tradition is teaching us, "Just as God lifted Abraham's eyes to see a ram to sacrifice instead of Isaac, so God is lifting all our eyes to see that not human beings but goats must be banished, must be offered."

God's Own Self has learned in these ten days to say: "A goat, a goat. No human blood shed here, no human blood shed there. A goat, a goat."

And then the substitution moves to another level. For two thousand years now, instead of goats we have offered up our words of prayer and Torah—by telling the story of the goats and praying insistently, begging that God move from the throne of justice to the throne of mercy. Instead of goats we have sent forth our deeds of *tshuvah*. The stories of the goats replace the goats themselves.

Our people put our sins onto the head of the second goat, the one they drove out into the wilderness, but today we see another way to deal with sin: "*Ashamnu*," we say on

Yom Kippur. "We have sinned, we have missed the mark at which we aimed." Tapping our hands upon our hearts, not harshly to make them harder still but gently, to soften them. Knocking at the doors of our own hearts to acknowledge the sin within. Not cast away, but owned as part of us, and thus confronted and changed.

The archer in ourselves, the wild wanderer within us, that part of us that would lift the hand of violence against everyone—how can we deal with that part of our identity?

The strategy of the Jewish Diaspora was to expel it, banish it, make the Jewish people into a holy people by abjuring all rage and fury. Isaac became the model for the Jewish people: Isaac who submitted to be made a sacrifice; Isaac who was struck blind by the flash of the knife above him; Isaac who became a holy victim.

The "normalization" that Zionists called for in reaction to the powerlessness of this Diaspora identity was both a political and psychological normalization: no more willing victims from the Jewish people, and a state like all the other nations. The danger was that in rejecting Isaac as a model, the Jews might become Ishmael in the traditional understanding of the story—in which Ishmael was the archer, his hand against everyone. The danger was that the Jewish people might adopt the unholy joy of celebrating violence.

But surely we do not read the story of the banishing of Ishmael on Rosh Hashanah in order to learn to become Ishmael. Could we neither banish nor become, but meet and integrate? Could we see the Ishmael part of our identity as our own, but as a part always to be confronted and transformed? Could we recognize that part of us that wants to destroy the Arabs, without succumbing to it? If we hear that fury in ourselves, could we control, prevent, hold back from what in our own actions drives the Arabs to fury?

Could we see their aggression as the brother of our

own, see them as very like us, hear their cry for justice as we hear our own? Can we let their tears and ours wipe away the triumph from our laughter, wipe away the mockery from theirs, transform them both so their laugh and ours can join in joyful celebration?

Then would God's final prophecy about Ishmael be fulfilled, as have the preceding ones: "In the face of all his brothers he will be present"—no longer an enemy but truly a brother. No longer would it be through a cloudy mirror that Isaac and Ishmael see each other, but face to face. And their presence with each other is from the same root as *shekhinah,* the word for God's presence in the world.

Could we also learn from the stories of Ishmael and Isaac how to reunite our inner identities, to renew the inner wholeness that was Abraham? The story of Abraham can help us to learn this, for it contains not only a prophecy of reconciliation but a moment of it. When Abraham dies, his sons join in burying him. Neither of them dissolves into Abraham, neither of them abandons his own identity; but once Abraham himself is missing, they are able to come to-gether in peace. What is more, they *must* come together in peace. For when the father who integrates both of them is gone, then their own incompleteness becomes clear. The jagged broken edges of their own selves cry out for healing. By seeing each other face to face they are able in a sense to create a larger Abraham.

It is only then, after Abraham has died and Ishmael and Isaac have joined to bury him, that the Bible reports that God blessed Isaac. At last he is able to act on his own: he seeks out his brother and learns from the moment of mourning together and working together that he wants to live together with Ishmael. So Isaac goes to live by the well that God had opened up for Ishmael and Hagar.

Must it take something like the death of Abraham to bring our two peoples together—some loss, some disaster, as profound for modern Jewry and for the Arab peoples as Abraham's loss was to Ishmael and Isaac? Some loss that would show us clearly how broken, how incomplete, is each of our identities—and teach us how to drop the cloudy mirror we have been holding and look at each other face to face. How terrible will the dread have to be? Can we not hear each other's cry of agony first, drop the mirror before the death of Abraham?

The peoples still sit looking past each other. Even those Palestinians and those Israelis who now accept that each people must be permitted to have a life and a state of its own on the ground that both claim—even now, almost all of them are accepting this only out of ironclad necessity, out of the inability of either people to control the whole land.

Too few Israelis and too few other Jews are willing to say that there is a Palestinian people, part of the wider Arab nation but distinct from its other peoples, that is *entitled* to govern itself in part of the land that is not just the "Land of Israel" but more deeply the "Land of Abraham," in which both branches of Abraham's family have a legitimate stake. And that the achievement of that goal will be a joyful moment for both peoples.

Too few Palestinians are willing to say that there is an authentic Israeli people with a deep connection to world Jewry, rightfully entitled to govern itself in part of the land that is not just the "land of Palestine" but more deeply the "land of Abraham," in which both families have a legitimate stake. And that the achievement of that goal will be a joyful moment for both peoples.

Both peoples sit unwilling to imagine that there might be a land of Abraham in which his two descendant peoples are entitled to be present, side by side, not dissolved into one but each with its own identity and self... each with its own self-determination... each complementary to the other.

Even the negotiations that have happened were on both sides rooted not in welcoming part of the family, but in the reluctant, heel-dragging attitude of doing only what was politically unavoidable, absolutely necessary: obeying the God of "must."

It was an attitude that created a profound vulnerability to the kind of impassioned religious commitment that led to the Purim massacre of 1994 in the Tomb of Abraham at Hebron, carried out by a religiously committed Jew, and to the mass murders of Jews by Muslims in Afula, Tel Aviv, Buenos Aires, Jerusalem. Over the years, I've come to feel more and more deeply that no peace grounded only in the God of "must" will last; that only when we have a peace that acknowledges and celebrates the God of "ought" and "possibility" can we respond without murder to the same deep religious and spiritual yearnings that became murderous in Hebron and Tel Aviv.

We have seen the limits of a decision and a policy rooted only in politics. So long as Muslims and Jews tell their different versions of the story of Abraham and his two families in ways that assert only one people is truly entitled to the land—so long will the peace process be weak, flabby, easily ignored. Even the "amended" version of this politics, a grudging acceptance of historical necessity—"We are really entitled to it all, but since we can't get rid of the usurpers we must make the best of it"—even that approach will find itself constantly on the defensive, always failing to satisfy the hopes of anyone.

But we do not need to be stuck in old ways of hearing the story. In our generation, we can hear it in a different way—one that all the parties can affirm as true to their religion because it accords with their deepest contemporary needs, as well as with their ancient stories and symbols. Not so easy, of course, to convince whole peoples and faith communities that an alternative vision, an alternative reading of the story, might fulfill even more of their yearnings than the older versions.

The new twist on the story is simple—and radical. It is to see that God—or Truth, or inevitability, or history, or the dialectic, or any deep force you want to name by any name—promised the land to both sets of Abraham's descendants.

Irony? Yes. God's jokes act themselves out in history, not in words alone. From this joke you could die laughing —and many people *have* died. Perhaps the joke is exactly why Isaac/Yitzchak was "the one who laughs," and why Ishmael was *mitzachek*—laughing-with-a-twist.

Perhaps they got the joke—which is why they were able to be reconciled.

From the standpoint of the jealous and possessive traditions of Judaism, Christianity, and Islam, why on earth (or why in heaven) might God have been so perverse and ironic as to promise the land twice over, to two different peoples?

Perhaps because the land that is called the Land of Israel, or the Holy Land, or the Land of Abraham, or Palestine, is intended to be a microcosm of the earth, and Abraham's descendants are intended to be models for the human race.

And since the great round earth has no boundaries chiseled on it, since the many peoples of the human race must learn in their very distinctiveness to share it nevertheless, or wreck it, here we are. In macrocosm, one earth, many peoples; in microcosm, one land, two peoples—two cousin peoples that must learn to share one land, one water table, one envelope of air, and yet be distinct and separate from each other.

A BLESSING TO THE FAMILIES
OF THE EARTH?

"THROUGH YOU SHALL ALL THE FAMILIES OF THE EARTH BE blessed," says God to Abram as God sends him forth to an unknown destination where he can more deeply become himself (Gen. 12:3).

So once upon a dream, I imagined the two branches of Abraham's family that share the narrow land between the Jordan River and the sea becoming a model for peacemaking to all the other families of the earth.

Has peace between them been easy to achieve? No. For there are no obvious boundaries between the two peoples, and they both feel deep yearning for the whole land each calls its own. Precisely because their journey from hostility to peace has been hard, I felt that if they could walk the journey, their path would matter to all peoples whose path is also hard.

For we all live on the great unboundaried earth, and most peoples love a scrap of land that some other people loves as well. In our generation of H-bombs and global scorching, the journey to peace has seemed hard—but necessary. It even seemed both canny and uncanny that the need for all peoples to make peace came due at precisely that point in history when two branches of Abraham's family met up once more in that tiny land where he had herded sheep.

To look on this crossroads in time through the eyes of Torah, to listen with ears that hear the promise of these blessings that would come to all the families of the earth: uncanny. To see this history as the workings of the God of Abraham: uncanny.

Yet those who look at the churnings of history as simply the efforts of human beings might see this moment as quite prosaic. For modernity brought the Jewish people to nationhood in the ancient land; modernity brought the Palestinian community to nationalism and a nascent nation there. Modernity had brought all the peoples of the world to the brink where transformation meets disaster.

So from these converging currents came the moment when the Israeli-Palestinian quandary over how to live in one small land coincided with the worldwide quandary over how to live on one shrinking planet.

The upshot? Have the families of all the earth been blessed by the behavior of the family of Abraham?

Only in reverse. A dream with all the colors reversed into their opposites. The green of life turned to the red of blood and fire, silver hope turned into black despair.

The two peoples do indeed teach many others. Ariel Sharon responded to brutal terror with still more brutality, creating an infinite spiral of rage and death, keeping himself in power by creating among many Israelis a hopeless dependency upon his mini-imperial vision; and look!—he became the model and the most dependable ally for President George W. Bush, a would-be real emperor, big enough to bestride the narrow world on tanks of oil and make perpetual war with boasts of Christian triumph.

It is not that the Emperor began his war against Iraq for the sake of his older, smaller brother Sharon, for the sake of Israel, for the sake of the Jews. The conspiracists of right and left who blame the war upon the Jews, for good or ill, ignore the fact that Bush has much bigger fish to fry, much bigger cities to burn, a much bigger world to control.

And on the reverse side of the historical phonograph record, a dark obbligato. Just as Sharon taught Bush, so Hamas taught Al Qaeda. The terrorists of Hamas pour blood on the streets of Tel Aviv and Jerusalem, and look!—a global band of Muslim terrorists learns to pour yet more blood on the streets of New York and Washington.

Can we find anywhere in this a blessing from the family of Abraham to the other families of earth? Is there any alternative to the war between Israel and Palestine, or the U.S. war against Iraq today, Iran tomorrow, Allah knows who next week?

It is not enough to say, "Put a team of UN inspectors in Iraq" or "Have a peacekeeping team of U.S./UN soldiers separating the two peoples in the Twice-Promised Land."

These measures might be useful but are nowhere near enough. What has gone sour is an entire vision of planetary connection and relationship. Treaties to make peace between Israel and Palestine, to heal the earth from carbon dioxide, to ban land mines, to create an international criminal court—all spinning down the sour drain, with too few supporters to make the imperial corporations and the one remaining superstate accept their authority.

It's wintertime for decency. But what dies in winter leaves, buried deep, the seeds of new and unexpected life. The one blessing of these terrible years has been the firm though frightened grassroots solidarity between some Israelis and Palestinians and some decent human beings from abroad.

Women who held hands around Jerusalem.

Men who together rebuilt Palestinian houses that had been bulldozed down.

Rabbis who helped harvest olives when Israeli settlers were shooting at the Palestinian farmers.

Israeli and Palestinian families whose very own children have been killed by "the other side"—joining to mourn both sets of children, all of them the seed of Abraham. Joining to mourn their children together as Isaac and Ishmael came together to mourn their father, Abraham—and by their grieving were released to live face to face at peace with one another.

Israeli soldiers who refused to serve in the occupation, and Palestinians who demanded that the suicide bombings cease.

Volunteers from Italy, Britain, France, and America who fed and healed and cried. And died. Yes, one of them—an American—died, crushed under an American-built, American-sold bulldozer.

These networks of resistance are not "international"—not between the nation-states—but transnational, crossing all the official boundaries just as the global corporations cross all boundaries, but with one difference: these are seeded at the grass roots.

These are the real seed of Abraham, and they could become a blessing to all the families of the earth. For the treaties that look beyond the old-time boundaries also need constituencies that exemplify nonviolence:

Germans and Americans who together will boycott the U.S. car companies that make SUVs. Who will put opaque "indictment" notices upon their windshields—for the crime of poisoning the earth. And whisk away on bikes.

Brits and Colombians and Canadians and New Yorkers who will "die" from simulated land mines in front of the offices of the generals and senators who have refused to ban them. And then arise to dance to the music of the peoples who are dying as these "leftovers" of war continue to explode.

Lawyers who will serve on unofficial alternative war crimes "courts" to cry out judgment on those accused of terrorism or torture or war crimes, to hear whatever evidence can be gathered, serve subpoenas on those who refuse to testify.

People who will not only march against the Iraq War but buy some food to be delivered to Iraqi children—and give the attorney general an affidavit testifying that they have committed this illegal deed of love.

Americans who learn from the Israeli-Palestinian circles of bereaved families to mourn all the dead—not only U.S. soldiers but Iraqis too—together with others could create funeral processions for the dying and the not-yet-dead of this war, group after group after group of mourners—with many, many coffins, each and all in silence, except for a muffled drumbeat, and everyone wearing black—mourning those who have already died and the not-yet-dead:

U.S. troops and civilians, Iraqi troops and civilians, British troops and civilians.

Israelis and Palestinians, Kuwaitis and Kurds, Egyptians and Jordanians who might be killed as the Iraq War gives cover to terrorists and vigilantes and armies of all stripes.

Saudi and Gulf States citizens who might be killed as a result of burning oil wells, depleted uranium bombs, and other long-term environmental effects of the war.

Americans, Liberians, Indians, Burmese, Venezuelans, and others who will die of hunger, homelessness, polluted water and air, and disease as money is spent on this war instead of on healing the sick, feeding the hungry, housing the homeless, protecting the earth.

The front and rear of the funeral march would display a great banner in rainbow colors:

SOME ARE NOT YET DEAD:
SAVE THEIR LIVES.
STOP THIS WAR AND THOSE TO COME.
NOW.

—〜—

Something, someone, died in these years of winter: The American Republic, Uncle Sam. And yet—What dies in winter leaves deep-buried the seeds of new and unexpected life.

On February 15, 2003, the great round earth, convulsing, gave birth to something new: A planetary community. Grassroots globalization. Millions gathering on every continent to assert that planetary community, not imperial war, should be the way to deal with dangers like terrorism and weapons of mass destruction.

These are the real seed of Abraham, who mourn their forebear's death and then join hands across the walls that are supposed to separate them, offering a blessing to the world.

WHEN MESSIAH BUILDS A TEMPLE

To the hills of the Land of Israel where the air was clearest and it was possible to see the farthest—

To the mystics' little town of Safed above the Sea of Galilee—

Long ago there came a Hasid, a member of a mystical community in Poland, journeying to consult his rebbe about a crisis in his life.

Struggling up hills, over cobblestones, through narrow alleyways, the Hasid came, panting, shaking, to the door of a pale and quiet synagogue.

So pale, so quiet that the pastel paintings on the wall and ceiling stood out as though they were in vivid primary colors.

As the Hasid came into the *shul*, he saw his rebbe high on a makeshift ladder, painting a picture on the ceiling.

The Hasid blinked, startled to see his rebbe with a paintbrush in his hand.

And then he blinked again. He frowned and tugged at his beard.

"Rebbe, what is this that you are painting here upon the ceiling? It looks like the dome that the children of Ishmael, the ones they call Muslims, have built above the rock where Abraham bound Isaac—the giant golden dome that they have built where stood the Holy Temple. I have just come from Jerusalem.... It looks..." He stopped.

The rebbe's gaze turned inward. "You know," he said, "here in Safed we can see and see and see... so far! And I have seen..." he said, and paused.

"I have seen..." he said and paused again. "Looking and seeing, they can be so strange. For example—our sages teach us that when the Great Day comes at last, Messiah will rebuild the Holy Temple in the twinkling of an eye. But often have I wondered: How can this be?

"Messiah will be extraordinary, yet still a human being merely... but now! I have seen... at the foot of the Western Wall, the Wall where God's Own Presence weeps and hides in exile, I have seen hundreds of thousands of Jews gathered, singing.

"Messiah has come!—and they are singing, dancing, as the Great Day dawns. Women, men, together—I could not believe it! The crowds were so thick I was not even sure whether Messiah was a wo..."—the rebbe glanced apologetically at his Hasid—"whether Messiah... well, forget it.

He continued: "I can see from the sun, the scorching heat, it is a late afternoon in hottest summer. Yet the crowds are wearing t'fillin [phylacteries]. So I can see that it is Tisha B'Av, the day of mourning for our beloved Temple. But there are no signs of mourning—except perhaps the way, the wistful way, Messiah reaches out to touch the Wall, to tuck one last scrawled scrap of prayerful paper between the great carved stones.

"I see Messiah speak a sentence to the crowds. I cannot hear the words, but I can see that from this voice there stirs a river—as if his words, like Moses' staff, have drawn forth water from the ancient stones of the Wall. I see a stream of Jews flow up the stairway that rises to the Temple Mount.

"The river of people pauses on the steps. They cluster around a wrinkled, tattered piece of paper, posted above the stairway. I see it is signed by the rabbis of that day. It warns all Jews to go no farther, lest by accident they walk—God forbid!—into the space set aside as the Holy of Holies.

"Messiah reads. And laughs. And tears the sign to shreds. The stream of people shudders—higher, higher.

"The crowd cascades from the stairway onto the great stone pavement of the Temple Mount. Their singing turns to the thunder of a great waterfall. They look toward the other end of the Mount, toward the great golden dome— the dome that covers the rock where Abraham bound his son for sacrifice.

"Surrounding the dome are thousands of these children of Ishmael, these Muslims. They are not singing. They are shouting, furious, stubborn. 'Not here!' they shout in unison. 'Not here!'

"'You will not tear down our Holy Mosque to build your Jewish Temple!'

"But I can hear the crowd of Jews—muttering, whispering, 'Right there, yes!—that is the place....No doubt, no doubt, the ancient studies tell us that it is the place.'

"Messiah is quiet. The sea of Jews falls to a murmuring, falls silent. They turn to watch. Messiah looks, gazes, embraces with fond eyes the holy space. Messiah's eyes move across the dome with its golden glow, the greens and blues and ivories of the walls beneath it.

"I hear a whisper from Messiah's lips: 'So beautiful!'

"The Muslims too are silent now. The stillness here, the stillness there—so total that they split the Holy Mount in two.

"Messiah raises one arm, slowly, slowly. The Muslims tense, lift knives and clubs and shake them in the stillness. The Jews tense, ready to leap forward with their picks and shovels.

"Messiah points straight at the dome.

"The peoples vibrate: two separate phantom ram's horns in the silent air, wailing forth a silent sob to heaven.

"Messiah speaks quietly into the utter quiet: 'This

green, this blue, this gold, this dome—this is the Holy Temple!'

"I blink. For seconds, minutes, there is not a sound.

"Then I hear a Muslim shout, see him raise a knife: 'No! No! You will not steal our Holy Mosque to make your Jewish Temple!'

"He throws the knife. It falls far short. No one stirs. The other Muslims turn to look at him. They look with steadfast eyes: no joy, no anger. They just keep looking. He wilts into the crowd; I can no longer see what he is doing.

"Messiah steps forward, one step. Everyone, Jew and Muslim, breathes a breath. One Jew calls out: 'You must not do this. You must not use their dirty place to be our Holy Temple. Tear it down! We need our own, the prophets teach how wide and tall it is to be. It is not this thing of theirs, this thing of curves and circles.'

"He takes a step toward Messiah, lifts an ax to brandish it.

"The man beside him reaches out a hand and takes the ax. Just takes it. There is a murmur, but the murmur dies. The man holds the ax level in both hands, walks out with it into the no-man's-land between the crowds. He lays it on the pavement, backs away.

"There is another time of quiet. Two Muslims reach out from the crowd, toss their knives to land next to the ax. The pause is shorter this time. Then on every side weapons come flying through the air to land beside the ax, beside the knives. There is a pile. Someone walks forward, lights a fire. The pile begins to burn. The flames reach up and up and up—to heaven."

"So," the rebbe said, "I have seen Messiah build the Temple in the twinkling of an eye. And that is why I am painting this dome upon our ceiling."

The visitor took a breath again. "But why?" he said. "Why would Messiah do this dreadful thing?"

The rebbe put his arm around his Hasid's shoulder.

"You still don't see?" he said. "Even here in Safed, you still don't see? I think Messiah had four reasons:

"First for the sake of Abraham's two families.

"Second for the sake of the spirals in the dome.

"Third for the sake of the rock beneath the dome.

"And fourth for the sake of the twinkling of an eye!"

"And Rebbe," asked the Hasid, "why did the people burn their weapons?"

"For the sake of the burnt offering. It is written that when the Temple is rebuilt, there must be burnt offerings. And it is also written, 'Choose!'

"Choose what? Choose what to burn:

"Each other, and the Temple, yet again?

"Or—the things we use to burn each other with?"

"So . . ." said the Hasid, ". . . dear Rebbe—you are saying that the dome—it really is our Temple?

"Forgive me, Rebbe, but I wonder whether the Temple may be the empty space—the empty space where the offering went up in flames to heaven.

"The empty space between them, where they burned the weapons—perhaps that is the Temple?

"Ours *and* theirs?"

The rebbe turned, astonished, to gaze more deeply into the Hasid's eyes.

"I see!" said the Rebbe.

And then together, each with an arm around the other's shoulder, they walked to where their eyes could look:

Far, far beyond the hills, much farther than the Sea of Galilee.

This piece was coauthored by Arthur Ocean Waskow and Phyllis Ocean Berman.

PART II

CHRISTIAN INTERPRETATIONS OF ABRAHAM'S JOURNEY

JOAN CHITTISTER, OSB

A Christian Looks at the Middle East through the Lens of Genesis

THE WORLD KNOWS ONLY TOO CLEARLY, IT SEEMS, WHAT IT is that divides the Jews and Arabs of modern Israel/ Palestine. What most of the world fails to understand, perhaps, is what it is, if anything, that also holds them together.

Ironically, what binds these peoples together is exactly what is driving them apart.

And yet, at the same time, it is precisely what drives them apart that may hold the key to bringing them together again.

Whatever the political divides of the time, it is the Bible, the spiritual legacy of Jews, Muslims, and Christians, in which lies both an explanation of the present problem and whatever hope there is of finding precedents for its solution.

As a Christian, I admit that my own judgment of the

present political situation in the Middle East is colored by this spiritual filter as well. These reflections of mine that follow, then, are my attempt not only to understand the root of the present tensions but to find hints in this common biblical background that might, if taken seriously, also provide models for its resolution.

The story of Abraham in the book of Genesis is actually the biblical story of the origin of these two peoples and the land they struggle to share.

Genesis is, in outline, a simple book, not unlike the primitive history of many peoples: First, Abram and Sarai are called by God to set out for the land of Canaan; then they sojourn in Egypt for the course of a famine in Canaan; afterward, Abraham and Lot, his nephew, leave Egypt and take possession of separate territories, Abraham in Canaan, Lot in Sodom. But as they settle in their new lands, Sodom is captured, and Abraham rescues Lot and his family when they are taken as part of the spoils of war. Later, Ishmael, child of the maidservant Hagar and Abraham, is born; Sodom is destroyed; and then Isaac, child of Sarah and Abraham, is born, and Sarah requires Abraham, in deference to her, to drive Ishmael and Hagar out into the desert, where God sends angels to save them. Finally, Isaac is also rescued by God from sacrifice.

Underneath the very simple chronology of the text, however, runs a different dynamic than time. Here emerge the characters, the virtues, the struggles, the hopes, the heroes, the sins—and the eternal questions—of these peoples who, God promises in Genesis, will each "become a great nation."

In a way, Arab and Jew, no less than I, may fail to understand completely the underlying themes of the story as well. Who is really the firstborn here—and does it make any difference? How are disputes resolved here? What great character flaws are exposed? What great strengths of character, in the midst of great differences, are displayed? Whose side is God on?

This segment of the book is an attempt to mine the implications of those elements, to reflect on their meaning for us now.

As cochair of the Women's Global Peace Initiative, a UN partnership organization, I have been working for almost four years with other women religious figures—an ordained Protestant clergywoman, a Buddhist nun, an Islamic scholar, an Orthodox Jew, and a Hindu nun—to bring Arab and Israeli women together in common cause. In all these experiences, I found myself viewing the present through the scrim of the book of Genesis. In my encounters with these women in Israel and Palestine, I have seen both the difficulties of peacemaking here and the scriptural hope that it is possible. These vignettes are the fruit of that reflection.

No doubt about it, I have learned a great deal from these women. I have been challenged by them to doubt the durability of political promises, but at the same time I have come—as a result of their dogged commitment to the spiritual history that both divides and binds them—to put even more hope in spiritual ones.

TO YOU AND TO YOUR SEED

Then the Lord appeared to Abram and said,
"It is to your descendants that I will give this land."
—Gen. 12:7

THE SMALL VILLAGE OF NEVE SHALOM/WAHAT AL-SALAM IS nestled on a hillside about twenty minutes outside of Jerusalem and adjacent to the fields of Latrun Monastery, a Christian Cistercian foundation. It is, at best, a strange and wonderful place at the same time, given the area in which it exists. What may be commonplace elsewhere, the integration of opposites—of blacks and whites, of Asians and Caucasians, of Jews and Arabs even—is rare in this part of the world.

Neve Shalom/Wahat al-Salam embodies what modern Israel and Palestine have not seemed able to achieve. Called the "Oasis of Peace"—a dual-language title drawn from the book of Isaiah: "My people shall dwell in an oasis of peace (32:18)"—it is a community of Jews and Israeli Palestinians who live in peace surrounded by two peoples in the midst of war. What's more, they live together in order to live in peace. They do consciously, intentionally, what the world around them finds difficult even to imagine now, let alone attempt. It's hard to explain why, except that maybe, ironically, these Israelis and Palestinians read the scriptures more thoughtfully than most in a region where it is precisely scripture that has been made the grounds for war.

Founded in 1970 by Bruno Hussar, an Egyptian Jew who converted to Catholicism and became a Dominican priest, the village of Neve Shalom/Wahat al-Salam was nothing for years but Bruno and a cottage on a hill. The land had been leased to the priest for the purpose of creating a mixed community by the nearby Cistercian Abbey of Latrun, a Benedictine monastery whose entire history has been devoted to the pursuit of both personal and public peace.

Years later, having planted the fledgling foundation and seen young couples finally begin to settle on the land rather than simply visit it, Bruno wrote in his autobiography, *When the Cloud Lifted*:

> We had in mind a small village composed of inhabitants from different communities in the country. Jews, Christians and Muslims would live there in peace, each one faithful to his own faith and traditions, while respecting those of others. Each would find in this diversity a source of personal enrichment.
>
> The aim of the village: to be the setting for a school for peace. For years there have been academies in the various countries where the art of war has been taught. Inspired by the prophetic words: "Nation shall not lift up sword against nation, neither shall they learn war any more," we wanted to found a school for peace, for peace too is an art. It doesn't appear spontaneously, it has to be learnt.

The question with which the village confronts the believer, of course, is a simple one, a direct one: Why? Why even try to put people together who come from such diverse political backgrounds, such distinct religious beliefs, such clearly differing worldviews and cultural formations?

And the answer is simpler still: "Then the Lord appeared to Abram and said, 'It is to your descendants that I will give this land'" (Gen. 12:7).

The truth is that the Arab-Israeli struggle over Israel/ Palestine is not about the blending of opposites. It is about the union of the descendants of Abraham as God designed it to be. It is about land given to "Abraham's offspring," to both of them, to both Ishmael and Isaac, one the son of Hagar by Abraham, the other the son of Sarah—by Abraham. Both legitimate heirs; both people of the land.

If anything, then, the conflict is not about a biblical mandate denied—"this is our land; God promised it to us," as some say. It is about a biblical mandate ignored—"I will make of you both a great nation."

The point, of course, is that these people come to bear witness to that promise. They come with all the prejudices, all the fears, all the cultural barriers they have been taught in their lifetime—about their own election, about the encroachment of the other. But they do not come suspicious, spiritually paranoid, absolutist or theocratic. They come to learn from the other the ways of God with the rest of humankind, to make room in the land for the other, to be peacemakers where others make war, to become bearers of the human community in a world riven by divisions.

What's more, they also come intent on making it work. "Let peace begin with me," we sing. The difference between them and those around them may be that they really mean it.

They send their children to the same school, taught by both Jewish and Arab teachers. They learn one another's language. They study one another's traditions. Like Abraham, Sarah, and Hagar, they raise their children together so that this time, neither of them will ever be expelled again.

They do not do so for economic reasons. In fact, the village has been supported almost entirely by others who cannot be with them, for whatever reason, but dearly want to see the village succeed. They support the village and its activities because, like so many others of us, they need to see at least a glimmer of something somewhere that reminds them of what is meant when it is said, "I will make you a light to the nations."

They do not live in the village for political reasons. Some have already lost children in the clash of armies that have brought no peace, but they refuse to continue to court vengeance as the way to victory. In fact, some have come to the village as a direct response to the useless deaths of their own children turned against one another by governments who argue for supremacy in defiance of a common seed.

And so, the promise of God hangs over—unfinished, undone, incomplete, unfulfilled. But there. It is not the message that is unclear. It is not the message that is lacking. It is the willingness of those who know God's law to live God's law.

The situation, then, is clear: the dictate "It is to your descendants that I will give this land" lives on still—this time not so much a promise as a measure by which the prophetic witness of both peoples will be gauged.

SUPPOSE THERE ARE FIFTY

THE VERY THOUGHT OF ARRANGING A MEETING OF ARAB and Israeli women in Oslo, Norway, in order to revive the spirit of the Oslo Accords was, at the very least, a daring one. After all, the Israelis might very well not be willing to come. Exhausted by months, even years, of peacemaking activities in their own country, with no apparent success, why would they travel halfway across Europe to engage in another one? What's worse, in light of a new spate of Palestinian suicide bombings on Israeli streets the whole notion of peacemaking was now less credible than ever in their own country.

On the other hand, it was unlikely that the Arab women would be allowed to come to such a meeting whether they wanted to or not. Getting travel permits from the Israeli government to travel outside of Palestine was at best frustrating, even commonly impossible. After all, Israel, heavily armed and clearly the more powerful of the two opponents, was not eager to have the Palestinian story trumpeted for all the world to hear. Negotiating with Palestine was burden enough, let alone having to negotiate world opinion at the same time about who was victim and who was victimizer.

So how could women even hope to make peace when the men of their governments set up laws to keep them apart? And on what grounds could they possibly hope to prevail?

"Our olive groves are being destroyed," Palestinians said, "and our agriculture dying for want of markets. Our land is gone and our homes destroyed."

And Israelis said, "We fear to walk our own streets. No one is safe. We live constantly under attack."

Then, two things happened that broke the Abrahamic scripture open once again for all to see, with all its power, all its raw demands.

First, a message came on the opening day of the conference from a woman who would have been one of the Israeli delegates. She could not come to Oslo, she explained. Her grandchildren had been killed in a bus bombing on their way to school that morning in Tel Aviv.

I shuddered when the news came. It was not difficult to imagine what an event like that would do to chill any possible hope for communication, for recognizing common concerns, for communal agreement of any kind between these women of the Holocaust, these women of the Intifada.

Here we were, spiritual leaders of the Women's Global Peace Initiative, at a meeting built on the hope that these women could recognize their common suffering and join in a common cause for peace. Here we were, trying to help women come to know one another despite the barriers that men had erected to keep them apart. Here we were, asking women to reach out their hands across soured political boundaries, not to bind one another but to bond with one another. And now what?

But the woman's message to the group did not end with despair or bitterness or anger. "Go on with the meeting," she pleaded with the rest of us. "Go on, so that none of our children may die again."

None of our children: neither Arab, nor Jew, nor Christian. None of them. Not one. She did not say, "Kill every Arab you see." She did not say, "Kill every Arab child you find so that we can even the score." She said, "Go on, so that none of our children may die like this again."

The message rang of a common scripture between them. And every woman in the room understood it. No one cried out for vengeance. No woman applauded another grisly victory over the innocent. And I knew why.

I remember my delight as a child when Sister read to us in class the passage that protects both the innocent and the guilty. "Then Abraham came near," the scripture read, "and said, 'Will you indeed sweep away the righteous with the wicked?'"

Then began the haggling that amazed and delighted me as a child.

"Suppose there are fifty righteous within the city," Abraham goes on. "Will you then sweep away the place and not forgive it for the fifty righteous who are in it?"

And Abraham cajoles: "Far be it from you to do such a thing, to slay the righteous with the wicked, so that the righteous fare as the wicked! Far be that from you!"

And Abraham challenges: "Shall not the Judge of all the earth do what is just?"

And the Lord honors the plea of the innocent. And the Lord said: "If I find in Sodom fifty.... or forty-five...forty ...thirty...twenty...even ten righteous in the city, I will forgive the whole place for their sake."

In Geneva, centuries later, those words in their ears, the women would go on with their meeting—and the one after it in Jerusalem, and the one in Ramallah, and the one in Jordan, and the one in Gaza as well.

In the course of all these meetings, the cry to save the innocent rang out again and again. The next time I found myself confronted by the living implications of the scriptures was when a young Palestinian woman sat next to me on the bus. She had come to act as staff for the group, but, I noticed, she came every day in the same clothes—all of them a bit too small, a bit too uncoordinated for the poise I saw in her. It was only toward the end of the conference sessions, on the trip back from a day of meetings, that I finally began to piece her story together. There had been, she told me, the destruction of a thirty-unit apartment building in Gaza the week before by an Israeli tank squad. The military had seen members of the Palestinian underground run in the front door of the building and out the back. So, they evacuated it and then destroyed it.

"I'm so sorry," I said. "It must have been very frightening to see."

"Yes," she said, "but worse to lose everything at one time. We're not even allowed to search through the rubble for our things."

I stopped short. "You lived there?" I said. "Where do you live now?" I asked, almost afraid to hear the answer.

"I sleep overnight with different friends, and," she smiled a little uncomfortably and pointed to the short skirt, "I borrow their clothes till I get some money to buy more."

"Are you angry?" I asked.

"Well, yes," she said, "but not at all the Israeli people. Only at the soldiers and the government. After all, their people are suffering, too."

The young woman was only twenty-three years old. If she can understand Abraham's debate and God's answer, if she knows that the whole city must be saved, if only for ten righteous, why not the rest of us?

DO NOT LAY YOUR
HAND ON THE BOY

THE MOMENT I SAW THEM STANDING IN THE CORNER
behind the table I knew that they were different from
the other women at the conference. There was something
about the look in their eyes. Something about the way they
stood there, some of them hugging themselves, shoulders
curled, some of them simply looking straight ahead, impas-
sive, immovable, as if watching the rest of us from a different country, a different planet, maybe.

The peace candle on the bare table in front of them
stood dark and lifeless, a kind of eerie echo of themselves.

"Who are they?" I asked the staffer sitting next to me.
"I've never seen them before." The young woman whispered the answer back, almost reverently. "They're the
mothers from the Parents Circle," she said.

I had been told about this group months before, but
frankly I had my doubts that the story as told was really
true. These were women, they told me, who had all lost a
child on one side of the Arab-Israeli military divide or the
other. The children from one side found themselves the ob-
jects of military attack. Children from the other side were
victims of suicide bombers.

The tit-for-tat war that was killing the young of both
peoples had become a long and seemingly endless struggle
between Israelis and Palestinians, brothers and sisters in the

faith, children of the same Father Abraham, but political enemies since the partitioning of the land by Western powers in 1948. Now, the holocaust of one had become the displacement of the other. The security of one had become the target of the other.

In a climate such as this, these spectral figures were expected to bring new hope to one more meeting of opposites who had managed to stay steadfast opposites for over fifty years. These women from the Parents Circle had been invited to the conference, the staffer told me, to open it, to set the tone, to bring people to the heart of the matter from the first drop of the gavel: children were dying, year after year, and to what end?

This conference on the Dead Sea, the fourth in a series of gatherings devoted to helping women in the Middle East make contact with one another in the cause of a peace the men could not seem to make, bore the title "Toward Justice and Reconciliation."

Nice idea, I thought. Easy for us to say. Yet, at the same time I doubted that anybody even knew what justice would look like in this place anymore. Who could weigh out and discover which of these people had really suffered the greater damage—those who were unwelcome or those who were unwanted. And how could the measures ever be satisfied?

Reconciliation, on the other hand, was not even an ideal here. Justice, maybe. Peace, of course. Reconciliation, never. How forgive the loss of land? How forgive the intrusion? How forgive the new rejection of one people by another? How forgive the lack of trust? How forgive the division of the ages between them? How reconcile the irreconcilable? After all, reconciliation had eluded so many groups—political, economic, international—how could we even hope to begin the process with a group as small as ours, and women at that?

—ᴡᴡ—

In this part of the world, even choosing the site for a conference was a matter of contention. The government of Israel permitted neither Israeli women to go to Ramallah nor Arab women to go to Jerusalem. Every Arab was a potential suicide bomber in such a climate, every Israeli a potential victim; every Arab a potential enemy, every Israeli a likely overlord, ungracious interloper, fearsome threat.

And yet, the women standing beside the peace candle in the front of the auditorium, some draped in chadors, some dressed in pantsuits, were a mixed gathering, some Israeli, some Arab. The Parents Circle/Family Forum included Israeli and Palestinian families, all of whom had lost family members in the conflict: Israeli mothers who had lost their sons in the army, a twenty-year-old Palestinian girl whose fiancé had been recently killed by errant Israeli gunfire, a Palestinian woman from East Jerusalem who lost her sister in the conflict.

But none of them spoke about anger, revenge, justice, or security fences. They spoke simply about the fact that it was the other—the mother of the Israeli son speaking to the mother of the Palestinian child, the Palestinian sister listening to the grief of an Israeli mother—whose presence, understanding, mutual grief, and lingering pain brought peace and healing to each of them.

All of them agreed that it had to end for both their sakes. All of them agreed that it was only in the suffering face of the other that they had seen the evil of the violence being done in their names, only in the arms of the other that they felt truly secure. Then they lit a peace candle and walked quietly away—together. Clearly, these women were light-years away from the political concerns of some of the other delegates at the conference, a lifetime away from the program planning of others.

These women had simply moved beyond the rest of us.

Clearly these women had all been to Mount Moriah. They had all gone, alone and together, to that place where it looked to Abraham as if it were God's will that Isaac be sacrificed for some kind of violent achievement of the inscrutable will of God, only to discover that God did not want anything like that at all. It was on Mount Moriah—in the face of grief, on the edge of the unthinkable—that Abraham discovered that our God was not a God of human sacrifices, no matter how seemingly noble the cause.

The Mount Moriah on which governments had sacrificed their children, their families, in the name of God had been for them, too, a turning point from violence.

Indeed, these women had all been to Mount Moriah, and they knew in their grief, heard in their hearts, what so many others either failed to understand or refused to hear. They knew, the hard way, that no political consideration—not patriotism or self-defense or national security—nor even the will of God was worth one hair on the head of one child, the real future of the nation.

These were the women who because of their care of one another lived through their pain to say to the rest of us again, "Abraham, do not lay a hand on the boy."

THE RIGHT NOT TO CHOOSE

Israel and Palestine are rife with argument. Every conversation wanders back, eventually, to one standard question or another: Where should the wall go? Should there be a wall at all? Whose house is whose? Who is building what and where? What kind of a building is going up? What kind of a building is being taken down? Who owns what? Who owned it when? Where is the boundary line? Why is there a boundary line? Who is allowed to go where in the city?

Every step is measured. Every brick is counted. Every life is measured by lifetimes—my own, my family's, their family's, going back thousands of years. If I owned it once, I own it now. If I own it now, I have owned it forever.

"That's the West Bank," the driver of the van told me with a broad swish of his arm. "That's an Israeli settlement in the middle of it," he added, as if two peoples who refused to be together were not really separated either.

The problem is that everything looks alike in Jerusalem. I couldn't tell one section from another but I knew that there were clear demarcations. Some people could drive one place but not another. Some people could go to school one place but not another. Some people could cross into Jerusalem but only with a permit. Some people could go into Ramallah, but they would be arrested if they tried to come back out again.

Every inch of land, as the psalmist says, has been marked off and the lines drawn. It is not an easy environment. One step outside the boundaries and you are liable to find yourself in prison—or worse.

My Palestinian cab driver told me that his brother slipped into the village of his birth illegally one night. He could not get the required permit to leave where he was to visit his sick and aged mother, so given the circumstances, he went anyway. When he was ready to leave, my driver—his brother—agreed to drive him to the village line, where he would slip out again as unseen as when he came in. But, as a roll of the dice would have it in a country of mobile checkpoints, the cab was stopped and the papers checked on the way. Because he was driving an undocumented passenger from another territory, my driver told me, his cab was confiscated and he spent three months in jail for transporting contraband. "Three months?!" I gasped. "How could they do that?" He sighed a deep sigh. "They do it all the time," he said.

A few days later I was in a village to the north of Jerusalem surrounded by high wire and watched by guards. "We can't go outside the village," a Jewish settler told me. "If we do, we will be shot at from that ridge over there. We need to have the wall here, too."

Finally, desperate for gifts and too close to Christmas for any hope of being able to shop back home in the States once the meeting was over, I hired another cab to go to Bethlehem. There, I felt sure, I could at least get small olive-wood Christmas cribs for the children. We had hardly been on the road five minutes when the driver made a sudden U-turn and raced off in the opposite direction. "Checkpoint ahead," he said to me. "Look at the line of cars. It will take us hours to get there if we wait for that to clear." I thanked him for trying and reached for my purse to pay him for the attempt, whatever the fact that I couldn't get to Bethlehem today.

"No, no," he said, waving my outstretched hand away. "We will go. Just not this way." And he roared off in another direction, straight into the countryside, up one side of a mountain and down the other. Finally, he stopped by the side of the road. "Lock your doors and stay here," he said. "I'll be back."

He disappeared up the road and out of sight over a mound of sand. Arab men gathered in clumps to stare silently at a cab from Jerusalem sitting on the side of a village back road with two Western women inside. I tried not to look back.

Then, all of a sudden, our driver reappeared on the mound, waved us out of the car, and, one hand at a time, guided us up the cliff and the hand-hewn footpath worn by a good many others before us. "There," he said, pointing to a line of cabs on the road below us. "We'll go in one of those." He exchanged car keys with a man below, ushered us into that man's cab with a gallant gesture, and off we went to Bethlehem the back way, the long way, the only open way for miles.

The situation was clear. Obviously, some people owned the land, and just as obviously, other people claimed it, nevertheless.

"Do you do a lot of this?" I asked. "Every day," the driver said.

Every day the guarding and the watching and the checking and the claiming goes on, down the barrel of a gun, beyond the guns, behind the guns, despite the guns.

But that is not the founding spirit of the place. On the contrary. Abraham forgoes the privilege of age, family, and power so that both he and Lot can live well.

Then Abram said to Lot, "Let there be no strife between you and me, and between your herders and my herders; for we are kindred. Is not the whole land before you? Separate yourself from me. If you take the left hand, then I will go to the right; or if you take the right hand, then I will go to the left." (Gen. 13:8–9)

Now, thousands of years later, Israelis and Palestinians are locked in mortal battle over the precise measurement of whose land is whose. The painful attempt not to be cheated is, ironically, cheating both of them out of peace and fellowship and trust.

And all the while, it was precisely Abraham's decision not to invoke his right as the elder to choose the land that would be his.

It is a painful lesson lost. The even greater concern is that unless both peoples discover that less can be more, the more of their rights they get—unlike Abraham, who was willing to trust the soul of the other—the poorer in spirit they will all be.

BUT HE LINGERED

I REMEMBER THE MOMENT VERY WELL. I SAT IN THE FIRST seat of the third row of a little second-grade classroom in a tiny Catholic school. Sister was telling Bible stories, complete with life-size posters of the characters. First she had shown us Adam and Eve, pointed out the apple and the serpent, flipped the page to give us a good view of God, and then, when that lesson was over, tacked the posters up above the chalkboard, where they would hang over a child's consciousness for the rest of her life. Adam, the arrogant, Eve, the weak, and God, the angry one.

This day Sister was telling the story of Lot, Abraham's nephew.

I loved it. First poster: there was Lot, hiding in his house while men banged on the front door. Second poster: an angel stands in front of him pointing a strong finger at the mountains in the background. Third poster: his wife and daughters cling to him, cowering. Fourth poster: in the back of the room, huddled together, are his sons-in-law, laughing. Final poster: a statue of salt.

Sister's message, of course, was that Lot is saved by God because Lot is full of faith. Lot's wife, on the other hand, we are made to understand, fails the test and is turned to a pillar of salt. She turns around and looks back at the past that Lot himself never wanted to leave, either.

The fact is that Lot is not full of faith at all. The angel

tells Lot not once but twice that destruction is coming unless he ceases what he's doing and leaves that place. Lot gives his sons-in-law the message, but they think he's "jesting," scripture says, and Lot does nothing about it. Finally, scripture hints at the real problem, not simply in Lot but in us as well. Scripture says, "When morning dawned, the angels urged Lot, saying, 'Get up, take your wife and your two daughters who are here, or else you will be consumed in the punishment of the city.'" But, scripture continues, he *lingered* . . . (Gen. 19:16).

Lot lingered. Lot kept trying to wrest the present situation, a situation that had sunk into irretrievable mayhem, into his image of it. He kept refusing to face the obvious. The situation as it now existed could not be saved, should not be saved, must not be continued.

Instead, Lot kept wanting to make things work as he wanted them to work. Lot lingered. He had to be saved from himself, in other words. From his arrogance. From his certainty. From his fear of change. From his unwillingness to admit that what he wanted simply was not working, could not work—should not work.

It's a common response to a bad situation—this commitment to making a thing worse by continuing to traffic in actions that are faulty. Rather than amend, repent, change, or leave a bad situation, we just keep on repeating it. Parents shout at children to be quiet and the children only cry louder and the parents only shout more. Husbands and wives continue to criticize one another, and the relationship only gets more sour when a bit of love might well have made it sweet again. Corporations spend good money chasing bad to push products no one is buying and so go hopelessly, helplessly into bankruptcy. And governments stay committed to domestic policies and foreign affairs that only plunge people and nations into ever more despair, frustration, alienation, bloody hostility, and centuries of simmering enmity.

It is Lot who should be the patron saint of the Middle East, that land of checkpoints and suicide bombers, of security walls and broken agreements, of adults who bulldoze the houses of the innocent and children who aspire to be martyrs. The situation there isn't working.

Only when Lot stops lingering and negotiates with God, only when Lot reaches out to make a deal, do things begin to go well again for him (Gen. 19:19–21): "Your servant has found favor with you," he says to the angel, "and you have shown me great kindness in saving my life; but I cannot flee to the hills, for fear the disaster will overtake me and I die." There is no bullying here, just respect and gratitude to the other and a statement of need. "Look, that city is near enough to flee to, and it is a little one. Let me escape there—is it not a little one?—and my life will be saved!" And the answer comes back to him, "Very well, I grant you this favor too, and will not overthrow the city of which you have spoken."

There are no demands made, no threats implied—and the request is a reasonable one: he wants only a "little city" and his life. No great mansion, no control of anything, no plunder or pillage or power.

It is a model to be envied. He does not ask for "settlements" in someone else's territory. He does not refuse to admit that the landscape has changed, that things are different now, that he will have to share a little city with someone else rather than live in royal isolation in the mountains.

The question for these times, of course, is where are the angels who will take us by the hand and save us from ourselves? What will it take to save us from the stubborn, but mutual, unwillingness to mediate what cannot possibly be won by force?

It is time for Lot to rise again in the Middle East, to be willing to leave what must be left and to share what must be shared. Then, and only then, as Genesis is quick to show, will the lives of the people be saved.

AND YOU SHALL LIVE

IT WAS A STRANGE CONFERENCE, AS CONFERENCES GO. HALF the delegates to it were long-term women political practitioners, peace activists, and natural-born enemies— Palestinians and Israelis who had grown up fearing one another.

The other half of the assembly were professional religious types—women rabbis and Sufis and ministers and nuns of all stripes: Buddhist, Hindu, and Catholic from around the world.

The topic, "Toward Justice and Reconciliation" (in the Middle East), touched every political issue in the history of these two warring peoples, both Israelis and Palestinians: education that accuses the other side of hate-mongering; business development in a place where people can't get permits to work; the healing of international relationships in a culture where there is more than enough anguish to go around.

Even more strange than the topic, perhaps, was that unlike most other political events of this type, this was the fourth in a series of such meetings. And every one of them opened with a day of prayer. For one full day, the women gathered to pray with strangers in strange words but with one plea in mind: the need for peace, the plea for compassion, the promise of mercy. Most interesting of all was the fact that the women said all kinds of prayers together: Buddhist and Hindu chants, sufi singing, Christian prayers, readings from the Quran, and meditations on the Hebrew scripture.

The room rang with readings from religious poetry and spiritual texts, then quieted for periods of reflection, then gave voice to private outpourings of hope and feeling from seventy to one hundred women. One after another after another. And no woman moved. They sat next to one another, the Arab and the Jew, the white and the brown, the religious and the secular, all of them linked only by prayer.

Later, a young woman from the International Youth Delegation, remarked, "The prayers at the opening of the conference helped carry us through. It created an environment in which we could meet and talk with openness and directness, and this is what held us together through those days."

Some people would scoff, of course. A situation like this is no place for public prayer, many would argue, when there are important things to discuss. This is a time for strategizing, not for religious pap and foreign rituals. Of what use could such things possibly be in a political climate, in the real world, in the meeting of opposites?

But it may be precisely prayer for the other that is more likely to resolve difficult situations than all the strategizing in the world. It is only when we pray for the other, see the other pray, hear the other pray for us, that our own hearts open to the possibility that these people are not out to destroy us. In fact, we begin to see that, like God, they wish us "well and not woe."

But can such an idea possibly bear the scrutiny of the Abrahamic tradition, a period in history that is full of invasions and armies and foreigners and fear? I think so. Consider the story of Abimelech and Abraham, in which the evil on both sides is clear and the consequences are major.[1]

—⚏—

After the destruction of Sodom, Abraham moves his herds and flocks to the extreme southeast of Palestine, dwelling in Gerar. While he is there, Abimelech, the king of Gerar, sees Sarah. Led by Abraham to believe that Sarah is his sister so that the locals would not kill him to have her, Abimelech determines to have her himself and takes her into his palace. But God, to save both Sarah and Abimelech, warns the king in a dream that his own soul is in danger if he takes her to himself, even if the adultery is done unknowingly. More than that, God sends barrenness on all the women of Abimelech's household, a threat to the very future life of the tribe, and then promises him healing at the very hands of the one he has wronged: I know that you did this in the integrity of your heart; furthermore it was I who kept you from sinning against me. Therefore, I did not let you touch her. Now then, return the man's wife; for he is a prophet, and he will pray for you and you shall live (Gen. 20:6–7).

Then, something strange happens. Abimelech reproves Abraham for his deception—and then forgives him and plies him with gifts and land. For his part, Abraham admits his deception, and, as God had promised to Abimelech in his dream, "then Abraham prayed to God; and God healed Abimelech, and also healed his wife and female slaves so that they bore children. For the Lord had closed fast all the wombs of the house of Abimelech because of Sarah, Abraham's wife." The scripture is clear: Both men have sinned. Both their lives have been threatened. Dishonor has been done to Sarah, and so deprivation descends on the women of Gerar, as well. But it is through prayer and blessing, not curses, that the evil is forgiven and the fear dispelled.

It is an Abrahamic lesson too long forgotten. Instead we rage in the streets at one another. We send bombs and bombers to break the spirit of the politicians and the hearts of the women and the lives of the young. We insist on our own innocence and refuse to confess our sins to the other. We will not pray for the welfare of the other and so we endanger our own. We will not make covenant with the stranger. We will not accept the stranger as God did Abimelech. We will not accept the sinner as Abimelech does Abraham.

But here in a strange land, with a foreigner king, Abraham goes on to negotiate the ownership of a contested well, the very essence of desert life, swears an oath of honesty and loyalty to King Abimelech, and resides there "for many days," the scripture is quick to note, "in peace."

But real peace only comes when a nation—like Abimelech—respects the other, despite the differences between them, and—like Abraham—seeks the good of the other and so swears to contracts that preserve the lives of both.

NOTE

1. The biblical story of Abraham includes another repetition of virtually the same story (in Gen. 12:10–20, discussed in Part I of this book by Rabbi Waskow), except that the king in question is the pharaoh of Egypt. Murshid Saadi Shakur Chishti comments on this retelling in Part III (see "The Brother, His 'Sister,' and the Tyrant," p. 143).

I WILL TAKE NOT A THREAD

DRESDEN FOUND ITSELF REDUCED TO RUBBLE. HIROSHIMA lay burned to black ash. Fallujah is razed to the ground. The oil fields burned daily in Iraq. In Jerusalem, gaping holes in cafes and restaurants and buses leave behind only a memory of the businesses—the people—that once thrived there. In Ramallah and Gaza bulldozers and tanks leveled the homes of those who built without permits they could not get and blasted away buildings that may, perhaps, have housed the angry, the insurgent, the incorrigible resister in the fight for statehood on both sides of the line. The question is clear: Where is the spirit of Abraham now?

I sat in the bombed-out café in Jerusalem where suicide bombers had launched a wanton attack as unsuspecting civilians hunched over the daily paper, drinking hot black coffee, eating bagels and lox. The café has been rebuilt, of course, but now there is a tight little fenced-in entrance in front of the place and a weapons inspector at the front door. To get beyond the iron fence to have a cup of coffee and read the paper in that place now, you have to show papers, be prepared to be searched, answer questions, identify yourself.

In Ramallah, I sat with an Arab man who, after working in Saudi Arabia for seven years to earn enough money to build a new house for his growing family, returned to Palestine only to discover that he could not get the building permit he needed to begin. Finally, with another child on the way, he built the home anyway. So they came in the middle of the night and bulldozed it into the ground.

He moved his large family into a two-room apartment, and after two more unsuccessful attempts to get the necessary permit, in a few more months, with the help of the "Rabbis for Human Rights," he built the house again.

Then, after the family had moved back into the place, they bulldozed it a second time. This time, with a new baby in her arms, the wife had a complete breakdown, the father had five children to care for, and the three younger ones were completely traumatized.

Obviously, Palestinians were not wanted in this place, so why give them a building permit? But the rabbis came back again, and for the second time they rebuilt the house I was now sitting in. The furniture was sparse, the painting was unfinished, the lighting was scarce, the mother was vacant-eyed and mute, and there was a pile of the old rubble still in the front yard by the one tree.

I struggled with the despair of it all in my own soul. Why stay with this international attempt to connect Jews and Arabs, to create common projects for Israeli and Palestinian women, to begin the long, slow process of making peace from the bottom up when there is no attempt from the top down? What was the hope here? Wasn't this situation between two peoples who, it seemed, had declared their natural enmity and cast it in stone? Weren't we all wasting time and resources that could have been better spent on other people in other places?

But then came the spiritual hope of the ages—a hope that transcended politics and defied the intransigence of it all. Here I was now, sitting in a hotel lobby with an Orthodox rabbi and a Muslim sheik. They had their arms draped around one another's shoulders. Their wives, equally traditional on all counts, were clearly old friends and we, Christians—outsiders—were all speaking a common language.

"No God who is God wants this," the rabbi said.

"We are meant to respect and learn from one another, to make the other free," the sheik said.

"Abraham, our common father, showed us all a different way," I said.

Clearly this reunion of peoples, faiths, cultures was possible. But on what basis now, in the face of so much death, so much bloodshed, so much destruction?

Too often we forget how Abraham himself practiced power, dealt with his enemies, maintained his own integrity in situations many would have used as an excuse for ruthlessness, a justification for excessive force. But the scripture confronts us with it always:

> When Abram heard that his nephew had been taken
> captive, he led forth his trained men, born in his house,
> three hundred eighteen of them, and went in pursuit as far
> as Dan. He divided his forces against them by night, he and
> his servants, and routed them and pursued them to Hobah,
> north of Damascus. Then he brought back all the goods, and
> also brought back his nephew Lot with his goods, and the
> women and the people. (Gen. 14:14–16)

It was a classic case of provocation and response: his nephew had been taken captive and Abraham went with his army to rescue him.

That we understand. It's what Abraham did next that baffles the modern mind, so sure of its superior evolution, its democratic heritage, its public rights and moral responsibilities.

Abraham routed the troops and emptied the place of goods and people. But he did not destroy it.

The king of Sodom came to resolve the situation, like

MacArthur and the foreign minister of Japan on the deck of the battleship USS *Missouri* in 1945, signing what would be the twentieth-century model of unconditional surrender.

And then came the surprise that could serve as a model for the ages, by one who sought to follow the model provided by the One God.

"Give me the people, but you take the goods for yourself," the king of Sodom said to Abraham.

But Abraham said to the king, "I have sworn to the Lord, God Most High, maker of heaven and earth, that I would not take a thread or a sandal-thong or anything that is yours, so that you might not say, 'I have made Abram rich.'"

Abraham routed the army but left the city standing. He took captives and sent them all home unharmed. He gathered the wealth of the city but sent it all back unspent. He restored justice but did not besmirch it by performing another injustice in its place.

In contrast, many Westerners got rich rebuilding Dresden and Hiroshima. Many get rich on the building projects and land that come out of the suffering of the people in Israel and Palestine. Many more will get rich siphoning off the oil of Iraq and rebuilding its cities. But this time, too, the people are gone; their homes and goods are wasted.

How is it possible to justify such devastation on the grounds of "an eye for an eye" in the light of an Abraham who returns the goods, releases the people, and says, "I will not take a thread of a sandal-thong or anything that is yours, so that you might not say, 'I have made Abram rich.'"

There is yet a piece missing from the kinds of political decisions that make people collateral damage and private wealth the booty of war. That kind of peacemaking cannot possibly resolve this war or any other. It will, in fact, only seed the next one.

HIS SONS ISAAC AND
ISHMAEL BURIED HIM

H E STOOD THERE TAUT AND INTENSE, THE LONG YEARS OF strain and pressure beginning to show. His answers were practiced but flat. It was 1983. Now Menachem Begin was only weeks away from resignation, a man who had borne the heat of the day and was beginning to wilt under it. We were in his conference room in the Knesset.

"They had a chance to resolve all of this in 1948," he said referring to the Palestinians, "and they didn't take it. Now let their own people take care of them."

"Their own people?" I asked. "Who are their own people? They have lived in Israel for a thousand years."

"They're Arabs," he shot back. "Let Jordan or Egypt or Syria take them in."

"Are you implying," I went on, "that if the Boston Irish had trouble with the political situation in Massachusetts we would have the right to send them all back to Ireland?"

It was a difficult thing for an outsider to understand, this division of peoples who had been one people for so long. But it was as common to the Palestinians as it was to the Israelis.

Some Palestinians had chosen to go on living in Israel, of course. They had taken citizenship there and accepted the new political state of affairs. For others, however, no accommodation, no recognition of the creation of a different political entity was even imaginable. "My family has owned this piece of land for almost two thousand years," a young Arab businessman had said to me. "We have the sheepskin to prove it. This is our land. We will not give it up now. Not to them."

"Them." The Israelis who had come back to a land long ago lost to them, after centuries of pogroms, exclusion, derision, and scapegoating and now, in this century, near annihilation, were interlopers, foreigners, unwelcome.

It was a standoff of massive proportions.

At the same time, the ironies on which the separation rested were legion. The two peoples, Arabs and Jews, shared the greatest holy place of them all, the Temple Mount and the Western Wall, on the same piece of property, one leaning on the other.

In Old Jerusalem, Arabs held the key to Christian holy places and had for centuries shared the city, divided into quarters—Arab, Jewish, Armenian, and Greek—with full awareness of the legitimate claim of each to the land.

Now the whole world struggles to understand both the differences and the sameness between the two locked in opposition, dedicated to resistance. The question is not an academic one. After all, the struggle between them threatens to engulf the whole world of Muslims, Christians, and Jews, all of whom lay claim to Jerusalem, the center of their various religious worlds. Every day the whole world gets up to the uneasy balance of the political teeter-totter there. Every day the estrangement grows more hostile.

But that is the political dimension of the problem. There is another undercurrent that runs through the system, has been running through the system for over two thousand years. The truth of the matter is that political exclusion will never be able to separate what is inextricably linked. The people of Isaac and the people of Ishmael, the nations of Isaac and Ishmael, are brothers.

The agony of Abraham lives on in them; the promise of God is yet to be fulfilled in them. Both nations are to grow and thrive in dignity, in confidence, in power. The scripture leaves no doubt of either:

> The matter was very distressing to Abraham on account of his son. But God said to Abraham, "Do not be distressed because of the boy and because of your slave woman; whatever Sarah says to you, do as she tells you, for it is through Isaac that offspring shall be named for you. As for the son of the slave woman, I will make a nation of him also, because he is your offspring." (Gen. 21:11–13)

There is, in other words, no choice here. There is no eternal division possible. They are heirs of the same father. However they grow, whatever they are, they are forever bound together. These are people who must learn to live together, if for no other reason than that's who they are.

Despite the fact that too many have forgotten that no political solution can possibly heal the ultimate bonds that bind them, not all have abandoned the attempt to heal what has been unnaturally sundered but can never be simply dismissed.

Abandoned, for all intents and purposes as a child, Ishmael is clearly never really forgotten, never actually disowned by the rest of the family. In fact, when Abraham dies, he reemerges in scripture, recognized as son, embraced by a brother:

> Abraham breathed his last and died in a good old age, an old man and full of years, and was gathered to his people. His sons Isaac and Ishmael buried him in the cave of Machpelah, in the field of Ephron son of Zohar the Hittite, east of Mamre, the field that Abraham purchased from the Hittites. There Abraham was buried, with his wife Sarah. (Gen. 25:8–10)

—ɯɯ—

Now, some twenty-one years after my conversation with Prime Minister Begin, we were still trying to bridge the divide, still trying to reunite what was essentially one people. We were in Jordan, and it was the second day of a conference designed to give a common voice to women from opposite sides of a common world.

One Palestinian woman after another, in one place or another throughout the day, had whispered in my ear, "The Israeli women have such practice at this. They are lawyers and parliamentarians and speakers and business leaders. They have to help us. We have to learn to do these things, too."

So that night I gathered a few very experienced, very articulate Israeli delegates to tell them the situation. "They are not rejecting you," I said. "In fact, what they really want is help from you. Can't you create interest groups and get them the resources they need?" I could see the looks on the Israeli faces. I had clearly said something very wrong. "What's the problem?" I said, pushing and prodding.

They were kind, almost tentative, in their responses. How could they show this American what she had clearly missed in the environment, especially since the whole purpose of the exercise was to bring Arab and Israeli women together? If it seemed they didn't want to help, what then? If, on the other hand, they rushed in to do such a thing, what then? The one who knew me best and could best risk being misunderstood, perhaps, said, "Joan, we really can't do that. It would be just one more instance of Israeli domination."

I frowned a bit—they had not heard, as I had, the plea in the voices of the women who had talked to me—but, disappointed as I was, I accepted their position. After all, there are so many cultural messages an outsider can miss in a situation like this.

It was the next day in the General Assembly that Abraham's voice came through in the conference loud and clear. The women from Gaza, new to the process, excited by its possibilities, began to interrupt the proceedings in loud, clear Arabic. "We want this to go on," they said. "We need to know what to do. Help us. Teach us," they called out to the Israeli delegation. "Why won't you teach us these things?"

I felt a hand on my shoulder. It was the woman who had told me yesterday what an impossible thing it would be for the Palestinians to accept Israeli help of any kind. She was biting her lower lip and there was a glint in her eye. I knew something deep and basic inside of her had been touched, had transcended the political, had looked beyond the Wall and the checkpoints and the land to the possibility that comes with relationship, with sisterhood. She recognized what Abram did.

Then I knew that the promise of God was still coming, must come, would come, was on its way: "Abraham, don't be distressed," God said to him. "I will make of him a great nation also . . . because he is also your offspring."

I WILL INDEED BLESS YOU

THE PROJECT SEEMED DOOMED FROM THE BEGINNING. How could we help Palestinian and Israeli women join together in a common project for peace, no matter how badly they themselves may have wanted it, when it was impossible to bring them together?

At every conference—Geneva, Oslo, Jerusalem, and now Jordan—the permits necessary to enable Palestinian women to travel outside of Palestinian villages or refugee camps had been denied. On the other hand, taking large numbers of Israeli women through checkpoints into Palestine was also impossible. Israelis were forbidden to go into Ramallah, for instance, for "security reasons." Getting into the Palestinian territories would be easy enough, of course, since only the passports of those going into Israel from Palestine are checked, not the papers of those going into Palestine from Israel. But on the return, Israeli women, too, would have been subject to arrest.

The only hope was to hold every conference somewhere neutral and hope that each delegation would be permitted to travel freely. They never were. At none of the conferences was the Palestinian delegation whole. Always, some of the women were denied the necessary permits. Always, the two delegations were unbalanced as a result. Always, therefore, the Palestinians felt outnumbered, unheard, unequal. Always, the frustration grew, the anger was rekindled and the degradation increased. The echo of oppression colored every discussion, shadowed every recommendation, blocked every Israeli advance, challenged every ounce of Palestinian trust. Surely it was simply asking too much. Surely the whole exercise would collapse in more recrimination and disdain than ever before.

Except for the fact that no one reckoned on the strength, the tenacity, the determination of these women, both the Palestinians and the Israelis. There was something Abrahamic about both of them that few outsiders could possibly have recognized. These were women who had each been brought up hearing about Abraham, the one who was asked to sacrifice his only son, or, more to the point, himself and the very meaning of his life—his future hopes, his present sense of purpose, his ongoing faith in the One whom he had been sure was God of Gods but now looked just like the rest of them, capricious, self-serving, bloodthirsty.

And Abraham did it. He poised on the edge of giving himself away by giving in to a senseless proposition that countered everything else this God had led him to believe. He took his only son to the mount of sacrifice with nothing but the boy in hand to sacrifice. Wouldn't it be insane to do such a thing? Wasn't it mad to go one more step with such a plan?

But these women also knew what Abraham knew: That "God himself will provide the lamb for a burnt offering."

So the Palestinian women kept making the long, hard journeys around checkpoints, by awkward routings, with long layovers, at great expense, despite the fact that many of them never made it to the meeting in the end.

The Israeli women kept in personal contact with their Arab counterparts between and before meetings. They worked through every channel they knew in order to find common meeting places in the border areas between them. They welcomed more and more Palestinian women into the process and called on international figures to provide the materials and the public support that such cross-cultural negotiations in dangerous times demand.

Each woman, like Abraham, sacrificed herself—her standing in her own community, her time, her energy—for the will of a God who had been with them all since Ur, through the struggles in Sodom, as beggars in Egypt, as sojourners in one strange land after another. Each of them was willing to sacrifice, too, for the continuing journey of two peoples into the will of God.

And so, perhaps, it was not so surprising, after all, to see that kind of Abrahamic faith and persistence rise again in Jordan. In Jordan, for the first time, a delegation of women from Gaza was also expected to be part of the conference. In fact, the meeting was specifically designed to be held in an Arab state for that very purpose. Surely Palestinian women would not be denied the right to go to a meeting on the Jordanian side of the Dead Sea. But they were.

Then, the pressure began to build. Israeli women called office after office to get permission for the women from Gaza to attend. The answer out of every ministry was the same: No. No. No. No.

Clearly, we would have to go on again without them. As organizers, we accepted the inevitable. Truly God would have to provide a ram in the bush, or else the whole conference could fail. Israeli women did not have to come here to have a meeting, after all. And without an equal number of Palestinian women with whom to meet, why bother?

But one Israeli woman refused to give up. Amit is a small woman, but one of the greatest citizens of the universe I have ever known. She goes into Palestinian territory regularly to help those women organize themselves, to teach, to create programs, to make the human contacts that make hate and fear and war impossible. She simply would not take no for an answer.

Amit didn't stop at the desks of the bureaucrats. She went instead to the office of the chief military commander in the area. "Let these people go," she said. And he did.

On the morning the conference opened, the word came: the Palestinians would be arriving late—but they would be arriving.

When they walked into the hall to the cheers of every woman there, Arabs and Israelis, there was a new kind of bonding, a renewed faith in the air. Why? Because they knew now without doubt that there was someone else who insisted on believing that God would be God, that any sacrifice was worth it to do the will of God for both peoples, that negotiations between them could happen and peace could come. In them, the story of Abraham lived on: nothing was sacrificed, except those things that need to be sacrificed if peace is to come—doubt, arrogance, resignation to the worst, commitment to anything other than the will of God.

The words ran through my mind:

> The angel of the Lord called to Abraham a second
> time from heaven, and said, "By myself I have sworn, says
> the Lord: Because you have done this, and have not withheld
> your son, your only son, I will indeed bless you, and I will
> make your offspring as numerous as the stars of heaven and
> as the sand that is on the seashore. And your offspring shall
> possess the gate of their enemies, and by your offspring
> shall all the nations of the earth gain blessing for themselves,
> because you have obeyed my voice." (Gen. 22:15–18)

Surely peace can come to a people who live by the words of such a God—if they each sacrifice something of themselves to bring it.

BLAME ENOUGH TO GO AROUND

"YOU DIDN'T SHOW PICTURES OF THE BUS BOMBING victims," an Israeli woman yelled out of the dark to the Palestinian presenter.

"I am just presenting our situation," the presenter returned. "You can show anything you want."

The roars in the auditorium got louder by the call. The "competition of lamentations" had begun, each woman remembering her own victimization, each proclaiming the injustice of the other, each wanting justice before reconciliation rather than the kind of reconciliation that leads to justice.

Where would we go to find a blessing here, a light through the darkness, an opening in the clouds?

Perhaps the only answer was to stand again and look from a great distance at another period, not completely unlike our own. Perhaps the only answer was to look at the first of the conflicts over land and kinspeople and relationships.

Maybe only Abraham could guide us back to our best selves.

The story of Abraham is simple and wildly complex at the same time. At one level it is the story of great human responses to the Great God of All, at the highest level of human theology, at the deepest level of the human spirit.

These people of Abraham have discerned the presence of God in life and cling to it desperately, through good times and bad, in the face of unbelievable pressure and with the conscious awareness of their great calling. This is the stuff of odes and epics, of great heroes of mythical proportions, of a love affair between the human and the divine.

At the same time, the story of Abraham is even more about God's hope, God's patience, and God's ways with a weak, stumbling, recalcitrant people who under no circumstances will ever be able to meet and match even their own best impulses, let alone the will of God Most High for them.

The story of Abraham is an oratorio of triumphs, a litany of failures. Abraham not only lies to save his own life in a foreign country where he might easily be killed by any man who wants Sarah for himself but puts both Abimelech and Sarah into danger as well. Abimelech risks moral death by mistakenly fancying Sarah, who is already married to Abraham. Sarah is at risk because Abraham leaves her at the mercy of Abimelech.

But God saves them all. God comes to Abimelech in a dream to warn him of the moral danger that threatens him. As a result, Sarah is released from the palace, and Abraham is forgiven his deception through the largesse of a pagan king.

Then Abraham risks his own life and fortune by making war against the conquerors of Sodom and capturers of Lot. And God saves them all from their weakness again.

Lot pays no attention to the warning of the angel about impending destruction and has to be pulled out of the place physically. And God saves him.

Then Abraham ends up having to divide the land that God had promised him in order to resettle Lot and separate the feuding herders.

And if all of that weren't enough, Abraham begets Ishmael and then agrees to drive him out rather than suffer competition between either the two boys—or the two women.

Sarah, mother of the new covenant, has all the signs of a small-minded woman, however much her historic greatness—too proud to admit that Ishmael was first born. Hagar, maidservant to Sarah, perhaps, but mother of the first-born child, from whom that other "great nation" would rise, was haughty and overbearing, uppity and smug.

And Abraham, though deeply distressed by the situation, gave in to Sarah, drove Hagar and Ishmael out into the desert with nothing but a small bottle of water to sustain them. And God rescued them, too.

The story of Abraham is one struggle after another, one mistake after another, one conflict after another, one sinful rebellion after another—and one divine rescue after another.

The story of Abraham is a story of deception, shame, fear, and faithlessness in men and women alike, both chosen and not. If anything, some of the best characters in the telling are not the children of Israel, the chosen ones, at all. They are the pagans, the foreigners, the unbelievers: the king of Sodom, the priest Melchizedek, and King Abimelech.

So what can such a narrative have to say to us about our own situation today, our own lack of care for the other, our own foolish and deadly overreactions to those who disagree with us, our own violent responses to those who threaten us? We are all to blame. No one is sinless. Everyone must repent.

We must repent the bombings and we must repent the checkpoints. We must repent the refusal to share and the refusal to receive one another honorably. We must repent the pride that leads to closed-mindedness and the closed-mindedness that leads to violence. We must repent our lack of repentance for all the innocent dead, all the lost relationships, all the waste of resources, all the lies, all the incitement, all the oppression, all the separation, all the ambition, all the force, and all the dissimulation it takes to keep two peoples who do not know each other hating each other.

We must repent all our false-heartedness so that God can rescue us again, as God rescued Abraham, Sarah, Abimelech, Lot, Hagar, Isaac, and Ishmael from their own small designs, their own great weaknesses, their own incipient disregard for the other. Then, perhaps, we will come to see what has been there all along: God's will and God's goodness working through all of us.

At the very moment of total desolation, the scripture tells us, God can deliver us from our lowest selves, too. If only we will listen to the call to accept where we are together and move on. Scripture reads:

> When the water in the skin was gone, she cast the child under one of the bushes. Then she went and sat down opposite him a good way off, about the distance of a bowshot; for she said, "Do not let me look on the death of the child." And as she sat opposite him, she lifted up her voice and wept. And God heard the voice of the boy; and the angel of God called to Hagar from heaven, and said to her, "What troubles you, Hagar? Do not be afraid; for God has heard the voice of the boy where he is. Come, lift up the boy and hold him fast with your hand, for I will make a great nation of him." Then God opened her eyes and she saw a well of water. She went, and filled the skin with water, and gave the boy a drink. God was with the boy, and he grew up; he lived in the wilderness, and became an expert with the bow. (Gen. 21:15–20)

Back in Jordan, the assembly called for order, the shouting stopped on both sides, the narratives began, the mutual suffering was recognized, and, in a conference that was meant to be the last of the series, representatives of both sides called for another conference the next year, but this time in Gaza.

Without doubt, God rescued us, too.

PART III

MUSLIM INTERPRETATIONS OF ABRAHAM'S JOURNEY

Murshid Saadi Shakur Chishti

The Stories Today: A Muslim Perspective

IN THE ISLAMIC TRADITIONS THE STORIES ABOUT ABRAHAM, Sarah, Hagar, Isaac, and Ishmael do not simply relate sacred history. They also form part of a long interpretive tradition, in which readers and hearers can mine the stories for wisdom that can apply to their personal situations or societal conditions today.

There is no one orthodox point of view on these stories, any more than there is one, and only one, orthodox form of Islam in the world today. *Sunni, Shiite, Ahmaddiyya, Ismaili, Sufi,* and other names are used to keep track of these differences, but practically speaking they may be no more useful in understanding an actual person one meets than are the historical, theological differences between Protestants and Catholics. As one could easily say about all major faiths today, there is not only one Islam, but multiple "Islams" in the world.

The perspective that I bring to these stories is that of a Sufi Muslim. Sufism is a tradition without a titular founder whose history is subject to a great deal of controversy, even among Sufis themselves. The word *Sufi* probably derives from an Arabic or Persian word meaning "wisdom." While religious studies textbooks and courses habitually label Sufism the "mystical side of Islam," the picture is far more complex and immediately begs the question "What do we mean by Islam?" or "Which Islam are we talking about?" As many people now know, the word *Islam* can be translated as either "peace" or "surrender."

One point of view expressed by a number of Sufis, in both the East and West, is that the Prophet Muhammad came to bring a profound message of peace and social justice as well as a mystical practice. This "original Islam" later developed into the organizational and institutional forms and divisions we see today. As I heard one Persian Sufi, who emigrated from Iran after Khomeini's revolution, baldly express it: "That isn't Islam. It's just politics and the culture that comes from it."

The Sufis, in fact, have many portions of the Quran on their side, probably more than do the more fundamentalist formulations of the faith. For instance:

> Tell everyone: "We believe in the One Being, and what has been revealed to you, and what was revealed to Abraham, Ishmael, Isaac, and Jacob, and to the tribes, and what was given to Moses, Jesus, and all the prophets from their Source. We will make no distinction between any of them, and we resign ourselves to the same Source of All."
> (Sura 3:84, author's translation)

> Sacred Unity has opened to you a way of natural religion. It was given to Noah to follow. It is the same faith that we have revealed to you, and which we showed to Abraham,

to Moses, to Jesus, to the end that true religion might continue in the earth. Don't divide yourself into sects: the true
religion unites all. (Sura 42:13, author's translation)

Reading the Quran, a Sufi finds that a great deal of it
focuses on celebrations of cosmic beginnings. It does not
view this creation as a onetime event, but rather as a process
that is still going on. In this sense, the Quran expresses
ideas compatible with spiritual views of evolution proposed
by contemporary Jewish and Christian theologians. Like
other ancient Semitic languages such as Hebrew and Ara-
maic, Arabic views past history as ongoing, receding into
the horizon ahead of us, so to speak, as the future comes
along behind us. For the Sufi, as for many Jewish and Christian mystics, the cosmic beginning of the caravan of creation can include us at any moment in which we sense our
divine purpose in life opening up ahead of us.

The Quran balances the ever-present experience of creation's possibility with the experience of judgment, of reap-
ing the consequences of our actions here and now. In this
sense, "time begins" at any moment that we live in attune-
ment with our divine purpose, the process of becoming.
"Time ends" whenever some event causes us to stop what
we're doing and face up to the effects we have created from
a sense of egotism, or a self that thinks it is separate from
the One. In this context, the Quran frequently mentions
the "day of judgment" (maliki yaumadin). This day can be
any day, any moment, any small "death" our limited self experiences that can that lead us to reconsider and align ourselves with the Source of Being.

To a Sufi, all of these themes—where we come from, our
purpose in life, how we can best act toward and relate to
others—can be found in the Abraham stories. In addition,
Sufis point to the following hadith, which are part of a spe-

cial category of sayings of Muhammad (hadith *qudsi*), in which Allah speaks through Muhammad, even though the sayings do not appear in the Quran. The following sayings suggest that there is a very important inner dimension to our journey through life:

> My servant draws near to me through nothing I love more than the religious observances I ask of him. And my servant continues to draw near to me through extra worship until I love him. When I love him, I become the ear by which he hears, the eye by which he sees, the hand by which he grasps, and the foot by which he walks. If he asks me for something, I give it to him; if he seeks protection, I provide it to him.

> Whoever discovers their inner self [*nafs*] discovers their Sustainer.

In Islamic mystical psychology, the *nafs* mentioned above is a way of viewing one's inner self as a community of voices, just as we might view our outer communities. As these voices, which make up our image of ourselves and our thoughts, feelings, and sensations, come to some "agreement" in any moment, more or less of the complete self says "I" to a situation in life. In this view, life constantly presents us with opportunities to "know" our full self more and more completely. The goal is to fulfill the image of the divine we took on at creation, an image that asks us not to be "perfect," but rather to be nothing less than completely human, embracing all of the qualities of remembrance, forgetfulness, light (knowing), and darkness (mystery) that Allah does.

My commentaries on the Abraham, Sarah, and Hagar stories weave these inner and outer interpretations together. One level asks, as we might ask of a dream we have had: "If all of these characters were a part of me and of my inner self, what would they be saying or asking right now?" Another level asks questions about our outer communities: "What does this story have to say about my relationships with others in my life, or about the relationship of our community or society to those who feel unlike us? If today were Judgment Day, how would we act rightly?"

THE BIRTH OF A PROPHET

A PROPHET IS BORN UNDER MIRACULOUS CIRCUMSTANCES. Dreams and prophecies precede his birth. A murderous tyrant tries to kill him and in the process ends up decimating an entire generation of children. Angels raise the prophet secretly and preserve him until the time comes when he is ready to confront the tyrant. A tremendous battle ensues. This is a brief rundown of the various Islamic stories of the early life of Abraham.

Most religions seem to make a special claim for the birth of their founder, and in the biblical tradition alone, we see similar elements in the stories surrounding the births of Moses and Jesus. Abraham becomes a very important symbolic figure for the development of Islam. The stories about him enable the Islamic tradition to trace its spiritual lineage to a figure who unites the stories told in both the Torah and the Gospels with ancient Arabic legends about the founder of the Kaaba.

We can also see something deeper in these miracle stories about the birth of a prophet. In each case, there is an enemy—Pharaoh in the case of Moses, Herod in the case of Jesus, Nimrod in the case of Abraham—who has seemingly unlimited power and who tries to prevent the prophet from being born or to kill him shortly afterward. From the standpoint of mystical psychology, Nimrod represents the tyrannical part of one's inner self (or *nafs*), which causes one to become more and more selfish, incapable of any compassionate feeling for anyone or anything.

The tyrant within us fears the birth of another, more spiritual part of our being, one that would connect us to a larger reality. The tyrant part of one's self pretends to be God but only ends up perpetuating suffering when it attempts to maintain this illusion. The places in us that suffer the most are the "child" parts of our being—those that represent a playful and innocent attitude to life.

In the story of Abraham's birth, even his parents, Terah and Anmuta, are reluctant participants. They could represent the unconscious parts of the inner self that have so far just gone along with the tyrant within—the bundle of habits that has worked for us. Both these male and female aspects of the inner self can be awakened to a sense of conscience and higher purpose, but the path is not always a smooth one. Neither wants to consciously betray the tyrant. What they've been doing, the way they've been coping with life, works for them—on a certain level. Yet they are inexorably drawn together by the force of passion and, reading between the lines of the story, a slow-burning yet unexpressed love bursts into fire when Abraham is conceived. Often love and relationship, even if we accidentally stumble into them, ignite the fire of spiritual change. The Sufis say, "ishk Allah"—the One Being is passion, the glue that holds the universe together, the love that burns first and picks up the pieces later. We may regret it later, but in the midst of passion, there is no going back. The illusion that we are, as the English poet John Donne says, an "island" simply evaporates.

Even after Abraham is born, Terah and Anmuta are not capable of raising the baby prophet: they simply don't have any experience nurturing the sacred within them. At this stage, according to the story, we need angelic help—a sense of giving our lives over to something greater. This angelic presence connects us directly to a purpose in life, to "God" or the ground of Reality itself. Nothing less will do. Often, in Islamic mysticism, the spiritual guide provides this sort of angelic protection (or what feels like it) until the spiritual part of the self can stand on its own two feet before the tyrannical part, or the grasping self.

So much for a view of the story from the standpoint of mystical psychology. It's not enough, though, to simply imagine an inner tyrant and the birth of an inner Abraham.

To me, the birth of Abraham also represents the birth of conscience, such as what happened to me on the day in 1968 when, as a teenager, I realized that people were suffering in Vietnam and that the people causing it were Americans. I remember writing a very sincere letter to the president, absolutely sure that he must simply be misguided or misinformed about what was going on. Later I learned more: how to do research, how to ask questions, how to make a nuisance of myself if need be. This led me to write more forcefully, as a journalist in the early 1970s.

Then I discovered that no matter how much one wrote, how much "consciousness" one raised, human beings simply did not make decisions based on information heard or received, or even based on logic. I had to ask myself, "Did I make my decisions that way?" A human being is capable of holding vastly different and paradoxical points of view at the same time. We seem to have so many different voices within us, and our motivations are often unconscious. So simply nodding in agreement is no guarantee that I will act the way I intend. Learning about how and why I acted in the way I did immediately zoomed to the top of my to-do list: it was no longer a spiritual or psychological luxury.

After many years of trying to balance head and heart, inner knowledge and outer action, the birth story of Abraham tells me: the birth of conscience and purpose does not happen without difficulty, nor does it happen only once. Life constantly calls me to hear what the prophetic voice inside is saying, right now. "God"—or in Sufi terms, the heart of Reality—constantly urges me to more compassion, more justice, more peacefulness in my life. Yet sometimes that voice causes a great deal of disturbance of the status quo. So I find myself called not to more thoughts but bigger thoughts and feelings accompanied by real action, based on the experience of a greater reality we all share.

> So turn your face and purpose towards the primordial religion of the upright, the *hanif*—the nature innately formed by the One Reality in which the One created humanity. Let there be no change in this work created by the One. This religion is self-subsisting, the standard, always resurrecting itself. But most among humanity do not understand. Turn to and remain conscious only of the One, remaining constant in prayer. Don't deify anything else in your life, not concepts or beliefs. Don't divide yourselves into sects that congratulate themselves on their own ideas. (Sura 30:30–32)

STARGAZING

When the night covered him over, he saw a star:
He said: "This is my Lord."
But when it set, he said: "I love not those who set."
—Sura 6:76

Then taking him outside, God said, "Look up at the
sky and count the stars if you can. Just so will your
descendants be."
—Gen. 15:5

ABRAHAM GAZES AT THE STARS.... THE QURAN RELATES A
pivotal moment in young Abraham's life, recounted
in an earlier section of this book, when he stays up all night
and successively looks at the stars, the moon, and the rising
sun. One by one, he realizes that all of them are passing
phenomena. Stars, moon, and sun set. He concludes, "I
have set my face firmly and truly towards the One who created the heavens and the earth, and never will I give partners to Allah" (6:79).

On the simplest level, some Quranic scholars see this
passage revealing a shift from many gods (some of which
were associated with heavenly bodies) to One God in sixth-
century CE Arabian society, a change initiated by the revelations received by the Prophet Muhammad. The Quran

also shows Abraham in a position like that of Muhammad, a prophet who brings his reluctant community a message of unity—that there is one shared Reality behind many manifestations and ideals of the divine. In the Quran, in fact, discussions and arguments between Abraham and his father or between him and his community over this point appear in no less than seven suras.

The Quran states clearly that the prior revelations to humanity, including specifically the Torah and the Gospels, also expressed the same simple truth: "There's only one Sacred Reality and we all share it." So it behooves a Muslim to compare this passage to the one in the Torah in which we also find Abram (before his name change) looking at the stars at night. In that story, God reassures Abram that his descendants will be as numerous as the stars in the sky, even though he has no heirs at present and his wife seems to be barren. And, according to the biblical narrative, "Abraham put his trust in God and this was accounted to him as righteousness" (Gen. 15:6).

Here, biblical scholars see an oft-repeated theme in the Abraham story—a concern for heirs, for continuing the line, and, by implication, for who will inherit the possessions he has worked so hard to obtain. At the time that the Hebrew Bible was being compiled, just after the exile in the sixth century BCE, these were important themes. Who were the real heirs to the tradition—those who stayed or those who left and returned?

In the Quranic story, Abraham sees the stars as a symbol of all that passes away, of all that is not reliable. In the biblical story, he sees the stars as the promise of a hopeful future, of what will remain after he is gone. Is this a contradiction? Is it just a matter of cultural differences that are a thousand years apart? Or is the One Being simply inconsistent in the way it sends messages to prophets?

—m—

Let's look at some other levels of this story, first a social one. What are the "stars" that pass away in our culture, the certainties in which we mistakenly place our trust? Perhaps we are not so deluded as to associate ourselves with our possessions—"you can't take it with you!" But we may have raised certain ideas that are no longer questioned to the status of "god," for instance, the myth of eternal economic growth and consumerism. Does a world economy built on the ideal of continual growth actually serve anyone except the most privileged in our society? What have been its effects on the poor and those who do not have the standing to be heard? Is individuality—"watching out for Number One"—an unmixed blessing when it causes us to overlook the ways in which we are connected to others? We are communicating globally now, in a world culture, but what are the values that we communicate? Like a star, doesn't even the Internet set?

Looking more closely at the story in the Torah, we might ask, "When we look at the stars do we see our descendants or do we see our ancestors?" Most people reading the Bible in translation don't know that biblical Hebrew uses verb forms that can express future and past at the same time—and they do so in the story of Abraham, the stars, and his descendants. "Your seed shall be like the stars" also means "Your seed has been like the stars." When we look at the night sky today, with the knowledge of deep space unveiled by the Hubble telescope, we can see light that left its source at the beginning of the universe and has taken eons to reach us. We could see this as light from our ancestors—from those who have gone before us. Do the stars need to represent only an expanding future—bigger, better, stronger, richer? Or can they also represent a creative past that is still moving ahead of us, reminding us of those who have gone before and, by implication, of our responsibility for those who come after—our children and the "home" that we are leaving to them?

Abraham gazes at the stars.... The stars gaze at him....

Perhaps in both cases, the light reminds him to listen to the divine mind and feel with the divine sacred heart containing his own, to consider both past and future. As another sura points out, it is all the same light, from candle to star; we only call it by different names. And so we sometimes forget that all of our ancestors and all of our descendants are part of the same family.

> There is no one but the One.
> Everything passes away except
> the face of the One.
> To the One belongs Wisdom
> and to the One you will return.
> (Sura 28:88)

A GNAT IN THE HEAD

SOMETIMES CONFRONTATION IS INEVITABLE. IN THE STORIES of Abraham's early career, everything proceeds gradually over forty years, escalating into a confrontation with Nimrod the emperor. Perhaps these stories link Abraham's early life to that of the Prophet Muhammad, who first realized his mission when he was in his forties and then spent ten years working with a very small community in Mecca.

According to Islamic tradition, in the Mesopotamia of Abraham's youth Nimrod encouraged every home and community to have its own idols, as long as Nimrod was considered the biggest god of all. During a local festival, Abraham's community leaves town and places him in charge of guarding the local shrine of idols. One might wonder: why does it need guarding? A raiding party from another village might make off with some of them and hold them for ransom, a bit like rowdiness between the supporters of rival sports teams today.

Abraham does the unthinkable. He smashes all but one of the idols to bits and then places the ax in the hands of the remaining, and largest, idol. When everyone from the village returns, he blames the one with the ax: "Wasn't me. That one did it to the rest! Go ahead—ask him." A good joke, but his community is not amused. "You know that they can't move or talk!" Abraham responds, "So why do you worship them?"

The idols of today may not be so obvious, certainly not made of clay, and Abraham's object lesson may not be so simple to learn. An image of something divine is not the thing itself. At best, a symbol, a word, or an icon reminds us of our connection to something greater. But when we lose the sense of what a symbol or word stands for, they end up being distractions. Today's most powerful, unquestioned idols may be words like *democracy* or *religion*. We think we know what they mean when we use them or hear politicians or religious leaders using them, but are we hearing the same thing they are? For instance, *democracy* has meant many different things over the ages. It meant one thing to the ancient Greeks, for whom it included only upper-class men. It meant another to the founding fathers of the United States, who didn't include slaves or women. It meant another in Central and Eastern European countries that called themselves "democratic" in the Cold War era. And the evolution of the term goes on.

Frequently, journalists ask me whether I think Islam is incompatible with democracy. I have to ask them, "What do you mean by democracy and what do you mean by Islam?" Neither word has only one meaning. There are many different Islamic voices in the world today, not just Sunnis and Shiites, but also Ismailis, Ahmaddiyas, Sufis, and others. Most Muslims are not native Arabic speakers. Many Arabs are not Muslims. You might as well ask me whether, based on a situation like the long-running strife between Catholics and Protestants in Northern Ireland, Christianity is incompatible with democracy. The West has simply had a couple of hundred years more to work on the project of democracy than the Islamic world has. For one thing, the Islamic world never had an industrial revolution to push things along. As a number of Western scholars have pointed out, Europe needed a more informed populace to fill an expanding industrial work force. This pushed the move to democracy.

My journalist friends also ask me about the seemingly more extreme portions of the Quran. Of course, scripture can be quoted for almost any purpose. So-called Christian rulers in the colonial era used very strange interpretations of the Hebrew Bible (of Genesis, for instance) to justify both colonialism and slavery. Or even in the twentieth century, interpretations of Paul's epistles were used to deny women the vote. The Quran can be used in the same way: take a passage out of context and spin a policy around it. At its heart, the Quran repeatedly exhorts its hearers to act justly toward the poor and disenfranchised. It says: "Beyond your petty tribal differences and glorified system of vendettas, there is only one Sacred Reality, One Being behind all being. So wake up and start acting like it!"

When we start to smash word idols like "democracy" and "Islam," which can mean many things to many different people, we need to ask what we're really talking about. Does *democracy* mean an ethical imperative that people should have a say in their governance, or is it a code word for enforcing Western materialism and a very modern form of global corporate capitalism on other cultures? Muslims in the Middle East, who may not be aware of the better sides of Western culture, ask, "Do free and fair elections have to go hand in hand with pornography, ecological devastation, and exploitation of the poor?" On the other hand, Muslims may also ask, "Does Islam mean a selective mishmash of cultural and political ideologies—the dividing theologies that the Quran warns against—or is it a simple tradition of peacefulness, ethical behavior, and surrender to the One Being?"

By asking "What do we really mean, what are we really talking about here?" we follow Abraham's method when he smashed his community's idols. We allow, symbolically speaking, a bigger question to eat up smaller ones, just as he attributed the destruction to the biggest idol. The point is that they are all idols, and none should be bowed down to unthinkingly.

Abraham's community can't go there. Even for his parents, it's a step too far. In one story, Abraham's father betrays him to the tyrant Nimrod. The biggest confrontation arrives, but even it unfolds over several gradually escalating scenes. First comes the miracle of bringing birds back to life, then the drama with Abraham in the fiery furnace. We could see these stories as symbolic of inner initiations (air and fire)—deeper learnings on the part of one's inner self. Something in life shows us that we don't have the power of life and death. An agonizing situation makes us feel that we're burning up, yet somehow, from somewhere, we receive the strength to go on.

At the end of the story, Nimrod sends an army against one man. It shows the power of one voice speaking out, or, on a psychological level, the power of the voice of our deepest intuition, which shows us a new way in life, against the odds. If Nimrod is the tyrannical part of our old, bored, selfish self, it sends everything it can to stop the breakthrough of the soul, of conscience and compassion in our lives.

What does God send in response? A gnat. This may be the Islamic equivalent of the "still, small voice" that the Hebrew prophet Elijah heard as the voice of the Holy One. Sometimes big gestures or large, outward shows of force only feed the fire. On an inner level, they only give more power to the part of the self that uses big, empty gestures, or loads of possessions, to convince us we're still alive. In this sense, expensive personal "self-development" programs are often only self-aggrandizement in another form.

The gnat crawls up Nimrod's nose into his brain and

kills him. It's a strategic strike. No one else is hurt, but it's not a good way to go for Nimrod. It would have been much better for him to surrender early and die a natural death. The lesson for us individually, or as a culture, may be that when the old tyrant within dies, there's room for real humanity and real relationship to be reborn.

THE BROTHER, HIS "SISTER,"
AND THE TYRANT

THE BATTLE WITH THE INNER TYRANT NEVER REALLY ENDS. The scene simply shifts. The egotistical part of the self reappears in many different guises. No doubt some amount of self-interest is necessary in life. However, when we take by force what doesn't belong to us or when we attempt to impose our will on another by force, the tyrant resurfaces.

Nations develop egos just like people. The original "ego" of the United States may be expressed by *e pluribus unum*: from many voices, one voice. The many voices are heard and, through willing agreement, speak clearly as one. The Sufi view of the soul is similar: many voices make themselves heard through the *nafs*, or inner self. They come together around a symbolic round table, where the voice of Holy Wisdom (which can be heard in the form of the spiritual guide or the higher soul, the *ruh*, itself) helps each to find its place in the larger picture. When the grasping mind dominates, masquerading as the voice of higher guidance or God, then the voices of the self are either enslaved to fulfill its demands or become slave masters themselves, dominating other voices. Such is also the picture of fascism masquerading as democracy.

Likewise, the U.S. Declaration of Independence speaks of the "inalienable right to life, liberty, and the pursuit of happiness." Yet the context of this statement makes it clear that both liberty and happiness refer to the common good of the whole community, not some individualistic right to take whatever one can at the expense of the common good.

One of the stories about Abraham, which appears in both Jewish and Islamic versions, warns against the tendency to fool oneself in order to justify egotistical behavior.

To recap the story: Pharaoh (and/or another king) hears that Abraham is traveling with a beautiful woman (Sarah). Abraham is afraid that Pharaoh will kill him and take his wife, so he asks Sarah to pose as his sister. Presumably, this wouldn't help Sarah but would save his life. The tyrant does take Sarah but is prevented from violating her by a seizure of some sort. In some versions, Pharaoh asks Sarah to pray to God to heal him, which she does. He finds out that Sarah is really Abraham's wife and criticizes Abraham for not telling him the truth. After a bit of back-and-forth, he sends them both on their way with Hagar, who is either one of his maidservants or his daughter. Most Islamic versions take the opportunity to point out here that Hagar is the mother of the "people of the water of heaven," a traditional name for the original Arabic nations.

Tyrants seem to always be in the market for beautiful women, as the story appears in some form three times in Genesis alone. Besides expressing some sort of ancient misogyny, what is the story saying? We can read any wisdom story, especially those in the Bible and Quran, as the story of our own soul. We are all of the characters in the story.

In this case, the self-involved or grasping mind wants to possess the female part of the soul. Although the mind alone can never really consummate its desire, it attempts to do so or to justify stealing the fulfillment due another part of the self. On one level then, this story presents the picture of what happens when the mind uses pornography to substitute for real sexual gratification. On another level, the ego of a nation (or of its leaders) can use all sorts of justifications to disguise from itself that it wants to rape and possess the beauty and wildness of another nation: its land and resources.

In the biblical (and Quranic) view of humanity, the first human was created in the "divine image" and was both male and female (Gen. 1:26–27). So we have both female and male reflections of the divine within us. Abraham and Sarah can represent these two sides within us.

In the present story the male part of our self, knowing that it needs to unite with the female self, becomes afraid that the grasping mind will kill it and take the female self from it. This feeling of being annihilated can happen anytime we become embarrassed in our own eyes. The critical part of our own minds (Pharaoh) can take on the critical attitudes or judgment of others (for instance, a parent or a teacher) and blind us to our own potential. We become afraid to take a step into the unknown for fear of our own inner criticism.

In this story, perhaps the male part of our being is that which represents our connection to others who have gone before us, as well as those coming after us. For instance, we can focus on our bad family or personal history rather than on a connection with a larger history of inspiring, creative people. The female part can represent the part of us that helps us create relationships to those around us now. The male side has a more linear relationship to those before and behind us, as in the proverbial caravan. The female side creates circles of relationship here and now.

When our Pharaoh-mind "steals" the female part of our being, it imagines that the pleasure it receives is only for itself. It is unconscious of real relationship. This creates paralysis. Healing happens only when the mind relents and allows the female self to fulfill her purpose by reestablishing right relationship with the male side of our being, our sense of purpose.

The male part of the self is also to blame for its timidity. By not standing up to the grasping mind, it allows its own purpose to be subverted, as well as that of the female self. The mind does serve a purpose in life—discrimination, clarity, and judgment—but not when it attempts to usurp the role of the heart.

Unlike the story about Nimrod, in this story, the tyrant doesn't die. The tyrannical self learns its lesson and gives the inner male and female selves someone to help them fulfill their purpose: its own daughter, a more enlightened part of the mind, in touch with the heart. This discriminating wisdom finds its purpose in service to the female self. Later in the story, this "daughter" gives birth to new capabilities that are in service to divine guidance.

The lessons on the geopolitical level may be just as hard to learn as those on the personal or psychological level. Most tyrants are killed by their own greed, sooner or later. The soul of a nation can be paralyzed by greed masquerading as defense or national interest. The circle of relationships with other nations (the female self) can break down, as well as the connection to the best of one's heritage (the male self), in this case, the higher ideals on which a nation like the United States was founded. This is what happens when the word *democracy* becomes perverted and masquerades as something meaning "you're free—but only to buy what we want to sell you and to provide the resources we need to do so."

THE MYSTERIOUS STRANGERS

Our messengers came to Abraham with good news. They
said, "Peace!" and he answered, "Peace!" He did not delay
bringing them a roasted calf to eat. But when their hands
stayed put, he began to mistrust, and then fear, them.
—Sura 11:69–70

SHARING FOOD WITH A STRANGER WAS MORE THAN A SOCIAL
nicety in the ancient Middle East. Before there were
many settled encampments, a traveler depended on the
hospitality of others. At the same time, a person who ate
your bread and drank your water was duty bound not to attack you. Hospitality given and received was as good as a
peace treaty today (and probably better in some cases).

So Abraham's fear in the Quranic story quoted from
above is well justified. Yet, they said, "*Salaama!*" and he answered "*Salaamun!*" That meant much more than our word
peace today, in that it implied mutual surrender to one
shared, sacred Reality, as well as to one shared Beginning.
In those days, when written contracts were rare, a word
spoken was as good as an action. This is why Abraham is
first confused, then fearful.

Perhaps for a moment we can suspend our judgment of
such customs as primitive and picture an earlier type of human culture we have outgrown from which we can learn.

Suppose, for instance, that instead of exporting to other

cultures the worst "food" we in the West have to offer—our materialism, consumerism, and pop culture—we exported the best: the folk art, music, and poetry that has fed our souls for centuries. Suppose that we showed people in other countries that we respected their own indigenous art and treasures.

Or suppose, on a very simple level, all meetings between Middle Eastern and Western diplomats began with a simple meal in silence, the hosts offering the guests not only nourishing food but sincere assurances that they would not seek to benefit by the loss of the other. Suppose that before laying out problems and programs both parties took some moments to breathe in a deeper sense of peace with the other, the peace that in both the biblical and Quranic traditions surpasses understanding, that is, our mental agenda. This is something that Abraham and Sarah might have done.

In the Quranic story, as in the parallel story in the Bible, we soon discover that the mysterious strangers are really angels in disguise (this is why they're not eating) and they're on two missions. The first is to destroy the community in which Abraham's nephew Lot has gone to live (and in Islamic tradition, to preach the message of divine Unity). The second is to give Abraham and Sarah the news that Sarah will give birth to a son, Isaac. Since the couple is already elderly, Sarah expresses a combination of both astonishment and consternation. Giving birth at almost ninety would not have been easy, no matter what the contemporary measure of longevity was at the time. In the Bible, she laughs. In a Quranic version of the story (Sura 51:29), Sarah hits her forehead at the news: "Me! A barren old woman!" To Sarah's astonishment, the messengers respond, "Yes, it's all improbable, all crazy, but even so, that's the message that your Highest Guidance—the voice that has sustained you throughout your life—is bringing now. That voice can discriminate very finely [al-Hakim] and tell you exactly how to make it work, on every practical level possible [al-Alim]!" (Sura 51:30).

Here again we could interpret this story as happening within our own soul, or self. The male and female parts of our inner self receive a visitor: a message from their highest sense of intuition that carries the numinous energy of the divine realm. This may happen in a dream, a waking vision, or simply a flash of reality in the midst of life that tells us things could be very different from what we consider normal. Sometimes the message comes in the form of a health or other crisis.

This message may seem strange or unfamiliar (as Abraham calls the messengers in one passage in the Quran). We are used to following what we have always done, within the limits that we have set or allowed others to set for us. We test the message by our usual means: is it practical, does it fit within our preconceived ideas of ourselves? It doesn't fit. That's when we start to become very afraid, because unlike a more superficial daydream or other imagined scene this message doesn't go away. We say, "Peace!" The messengers say, "Peace!" But it looks like our lives could be overturned entirely.

The message is twofold. Something is going to die: the distracting habits of a lifetime that keep us from being the compassionate, creative human beings that Allah intended. This is the community from which the prophet Lot (a small, redeemable portion of our old way of living) needs to be rescued. Something new is going to be born: a child from the union of the two greatest opposites in the self— our deepest purpose in life (the male self) and our deepest sense of relationship (the female self).

Culturally and politically, breaking the habits of fear and hearing the voice of the outsider are just as difficult.

Many of our political leaders marshal all sorts of reasons and rationalizations to convince us that Western countries need to protect themselves from "strangers" and cannot possibly be the beacons of compassion and peace that some of our visionaries have advocated in the past. There are all sorts of reasons given today why billions for defense cannot include a greater measure of hospitality for the poorest nations in the world, many of which are poor due at least in part to our colonial or postcolonial interventions.

For Abraham and Sarah, hospitality was the best defense. We could revive real hospitality with the simple realization that there is only one shared Reality, for rich and poor.

THE WELL OF ABUNDANT WATER

U P UNTIL AFTER THE ANGELS ARRIVE, WE DON'T HEAR much about Hagar, even in the Islamic story. In the Bible, she and Ishmael seem to be the casualties of a domestic dispute between Sarah and herself in Abraham's tent. Whether the parting of the ways between Hagar and Abraham benefits both parties depends upon how one sees the subsequent story. As mentioned earlier, the Islamic traditions give Hagar the possibility of a noble birth. She is no mere servant but the daughter of the Egyptian pharaoh and the mother of all Arabs. If we consider Sarah the priestess-matriarch of the family, then Hagar is her assistant. In several ancient matrilineal cultures in nomadic society, the priestess could ask her assistant to provide her with a child if she was unable to do so herself.[1]

Due to the encounter with the angels, however, we end up with two children, Isaac and Ishmael. Even with the best of intentions, it seems there is never only one way to fulfill the divine purpose.

In the Bible, Hagar and Ishmael end up at the "Well of the Living One Who Sees Me" in Syria. In the Quran, they end up much farther away, at the "Well of Abundant Water" *(zamzam)* near Mecca in Arabia. Like many indigenous cultures, the nomadic cultures of the Middle East considered wells and springs sacred. Stories were told about and around wells as travelers stopped to refresh themselves. Stories, like wells, connected them to a deeper source of life.

According to the Islamic story, the well near Mecca appears as a result of divine intervention. Abraham takes Hagar and Ishmael to what he admits (to God) is a barren place and turns to go home. Significantly, there is no report that God commanded Abraham to do this. Hagar follows and asks him where is going and what he is doing leaving them in a place where they are unlikely to survive or meet anyone else. She asks several times, but he refuses to answer. It's a tense moment. Finally, she asks him whether God commanded him to take them there. He answers, "Yes." She responds, "Then God will not neglect us."

At this point, Hagar's faith takes over where Abraham's (seemingly) erratic guidance leaves off. Her water skin runs dry. Ishmael begins to die of heat exhaustion and thirst. Hagar runs back and forth between two hills, looking desperately for help. Then she hears the divine voice, directing her back to the tree where she left Ishmael. There she finds an angel (or, in some accounts, Ishmael himself) digging his heel into the earth. Water begins to appear, then flows more and more abundantly. Hagar creates a small dam around the new spring so that the water accumulates.

Let's pause here and look at the story as though the characters were all parts of ourselves. For instance, the Abraham part of ourself tries but fails but fails to make sense of two different relationships or ways of relating to the world. Maybe we see ourselves one way at home and another when we are away or at work. It may be like two different people inside of us attempting to reconcile with each other. So we try separating them even further, but this ultimately doesn't work. Each way that we relate to life, each arena in which we invest energy and love, bears fruit—inner children—and they have a life of their own. These new capabilities and new ways to feel uncover wellsprings of new inspiration, creativity, and wisdom within us; they dig channels that open to the sacred depths of our soul. Eventually, at the end of this story in both the biblical and Quranic versions, it is the children who reconcile the two families of Abraham at their father's graveside.

The simple message of this complex family systems saga is: where real relationship occurs, expect the unexpected; "grace" always has a chance to rescue the situation. No matter how much we think we have life figured out, a great deal of mystery remains. Sometimes angels (or what seem like them) do show up. Sometimes it's the child part of ourselves, who through play discovers an entirely new solution to the problem, one that running around and being busy doesn't provide. Let's not forget that Hagar and Ishmael are dying of thirst. Although the situation may look bleak, we need to be ready to try something totally unexpected, contrary to logic, if we want our world to survive whole.

On the geopolitical level, the message might be: why don't our politicians and diplomats involved in situations in the Middle East take the time to establish deeper friendships, or at least deeper relationships of trust, in which frank self-disclosure, sharing of feeling, and a certain amount of psychological honesty are more prevalent? This would not require too much extra training, although it would require them to dig deeper to find their own well of emotional trust and honesty. Most university counseling, spiritual direction, or humanistic psychotherapy programs are less than three years in length. This presumes that peace—the completeness and harmony that are the original definitions of both *shalom* and *salaam*—is really what is wanted and not simply a term behind which to hide other agendas.

The story of Hagar, Abraham, Ishmael, and the well ties the spiritual lineage and primary sacred sites of Islam into the biblical account in a way that reframes but does not contradict the Bible. What seems like exile may really be the opportunity for an entirely new inspiration to arise. It need not replace or compete with the older tradition. In fact, as the Quran says, all sacred traditions essentially come from one sacred source. There's no point arguing about this source or about the ideas that we make up about it. The latter are just stories we tell ourselves in order to remember what is important and to allow ourselves to feel a connection with each other.

Together we can learn about the divine purpose of life through the abundant flow of diversity—the many ways that the One Being expresses itself in all the peoples and ecologies of the world. This is the real Well of Zamzam.

NOTE

1. For more on this interpretation of the story, see *Hagar the Egyptian: The Lost Tradition of the Matriarchs* by Savina Treubal (San Francisco: Harper San Francisco, 1990).

VISITING RIGHTS AND
BORDER CONTROL

O my Sustainer! I have settled some of my family in an
uncultivated valley by your sacred house in order that they
might establish regular prayer. Fill the hearts of some with
love towards them and feed them so that they can give
thanks. You know what we conceal and reveal. Nothing
in earth or heaven is hidden from the One Being.

—Sura 14:37–38

AFTER ABRAHAM LEAVES HAGAR AND ISHMAEL OUT IN THE
wilderness, his prayer for them is answered. A passing
tribe sees birds circling over the new Well of Zamzam.
They ask Hagar for permission to settle there and she
agrees. Yet, in contrast to the biblical version, this is only
the beginning of Hagar and Ishmael's story. As he grows
up, Ishmael learns hunting from the tribe and later marries
a local woman.

Meanwhile, back home in Syria, Abraham wonders
after many years how the Meccan branch of his family is doing. According to Islamic legend, Sarah agrees that Abraham can visit, but he must not dismount from his horse. In
some legends, he rides a special horse sent to him by the angel Gabriel in order to speed up the journey. He visits three
times. During the first two visits, which are reported by
early Islamic commentators but not in the Quran, Abraham

seems to act like a typical absent father, interfering in the life of his son.

The first time Abraham arrives he is met by Ishmael's wife, who is rude and inhospitable and doesn't ask his name. Abraham leaves a message for his son to "change your threshold" and returns home. Ishmael returns home, "smells the scent of his father," and changes his threshold by divorcing his first wife and marrying another. Predictably, Abraham receives much better treatment the second time. The second wife welcomes him and offers him a feast. Again he is not asked his name. In some stories, Ishmael's second wife also washes Abraham's head. He departs and leaves the message "your threshold is solid." Ishmael returns, smells his father's presence, receives the message, and then explains it all to his wife.

Once again we see the theme of hospitality, which we must remember was a survival skill in a largely nomadic culture that only slowly adapted itself to the idea of more or less permanent settlement. Possibly this story reflects a much older one in Arab culture, one that sought to convey the importance of preexisting, communal values, like hospitality, as settled existence began to spread. As more people gathered together in early towns, one might feel relatively safe, surrounded by larger numbers of people. Yet many people would still have understood an inhospitable welcome as an aggressive act.

Let's look at a spiritual interpretation of this story. Here Abraham acts like our higher intuition. Once the process of divine guidance is set in motion in the psyche (as in the story of Hagar's well, discussed above), it's not necessary to constantly adjust things, to "micromanage" the self, so to speak. So Abraham doesn't return for some time. Divine guidance takes its own course and grows its own seeds. After a while, Abraham returns to check out how the various "selves" are doing. The male self (Ishmael) is out hunting

—following a path of accomplishment, which helps it to develop various qualities and skills, in service to the One Being. The female self (his wife) is at home, minding the doorway. In this story, she controls the border, determining who can enter and who cannot. She seems to have forgotten the importance of welcome and is overly protective. If no one is welcomed, one makes no friends. If one has no friends, one has no protection. Therefore, her motivation is neither logical nor instinctive, simply lazy. When the male self returns home and finds out what has happened, he changes the border policy. Accomplishment (hunting) and relationship (hospitality) need to be in balance for life to work.

Yes, Abraham is a bit of a busybody in this story. Yet he only serves, as does one's higher intuition, to reflect back to the self an imbalanced situation of which it may have been unaware.

From the standpoint of a nation's soul, we can assess psychological and spiritual health in the same way. Is accomplishment out of balance with relationship? Do national priorities lean more toward profit and production than toward hospitality, at home and abroad? How well do we make friends with those we see as strangers? Do we have a good threshold, or do we make enemies from friends at our doorstep?

In another of the hadith *qudsi* (or special sayings through Muhammad) we find the following story, which is very similar to a story that Jesus tells in the Gospels (Matt. 25: 35–45):

> Allah will proclaim on the Day of Resurrection:
> "O children of Adam, I was sick and you did not visit me, hungry and you did not feed me, thirsty and you did not quench my thirst."
> The souls will respond: "O Sustainer, how could we

visit you, feed you, or quench your thirst, you who already sustain and nurture all levels of existence?"

"Were you not aware? Many known to you were sick or hungry or thirsty. Had you visited them you would have found me with and in them. Had you fed them you would have found me in the process. Had you quenched their thirst, you would have discovered me through this offering."

WHERE ADAM AND EVE
MADE LOVE

> We identified for Abraham the site of the House and told
> him: "Do not associate any thing, thought, or idea with
> the One Reality when you pray; and sanctify my House
> for those who circumambulate it or stand up, or bow, or
> prostrate themselves there."
> —Sura 22:26

THE CLIMAX OF THE STORY OF ABRAHAM IN MECCA COMES
with his third visit, when, according to Islamic tradition, he and Ishmael build the Kaaba. This time when
Abraham arrives, Ishmael is at home trimming arrows,
preparing to go hunting again. Abraham tells him of God's
command to build the Kaaba, and Ishmael offers to help.

A divine messenger in the form of a cloud or wind
shows them the site. As they dig, they find the foundations
of an older shrine, built by Adam. Here pre-Islamic and
nonorthodox biblical traditions knit themselves together
with the story related by the Quran and in the hadith. In
the larger Islamic story, as told by various commentators,[1]
Adam and Eve were expelled from paradise when they were
tempted into ignoring God's command not to eat grain
from the "Plant of Eternity" (a change from the biblical
Tree of the Knowledge of Good and Evil). They were
tempted to do this by Iblis (a rebellious angel), who said

that eating the grain would make them eternal. This telling of the story seems to reflect an early suspicion of agriculture as providing a false sense of security. A nomad depended upon the grace of the divine realm for survival.

After Adam and Eve leave Paradise, they are separated for hundreds of years, each mourning their joint mistake as well as their separation from each other. According to one story, Adam lands in India and his tears turn to musk, while Eve lands on the coast of Arabia and her tears turn to pearls and coral. The wind carries their voices to each other, which causes them even more sorrow and longing. Finally, when they have repented enough, God reunites them in Mecca. First they circumambulate and then make love inside the original Kaaba.

These older, evocative stories become part of Islamic tradition when the Quran describes Abraham and Ishmael rebuilding the Kaaba. According to this story, the famous Black Stone in a corner of the Kaaba was first a brilliant white, brought by Adam from paradise. The angel Gabriel carries it to Abraham from India, but in subsequent generations it turns black during disputes over who owns the shrine.

As Abraham and Ishmael build the Kaaba they pray:

> O Sustainer, accept this service from us, for you are the illumination of all seeing and all knowing. Our Nurturer, teach our children and us how to surrender to Unity, so that we may become a community bowing to the sacred in all. Show us the places where we can celebrate the rites appropriate for us. Return us to the rhythm that is ripe for us, for You are the One who returns us to the rhythm of Reality with unrestricted mercy and love. (Sura 2:127–128)

On a mythic and psychological level, these stories communicate important wisdom from the past: the overreaching of Adam and Eve trying to attain immortality; the softening power of their tears; the power of their longing for each other; and the birth of sacred space, where surrender to the divine combines with deep love for another person.

It may be difficult for us to peel back the layers of our modern intelligence to understand the importance of story, sacred space, or shared community ritual today. The deeper, more symbolic side of nature and creation has been replaced by a utilitarian view, which sees nature as an object to be used rather than as a living being communicating a sacred reality of equal value to our own existence. Likewise, ritual and story become something nonessential, at best hobbies, at worst a waste of time in our secularized, flatland existence. Time shortens and becomes embodied in series of to-do lists instead of pulsing in rhythm ahead of and behind us to allow us to connect in feeling with those who have gone before us and those who come after. Reflected on another level, immediate political and economic events and strategies become the only things actually valued as "reality." In this culture, even a spiritual story can be manipulated like an object, which serves to bolster various fundamentalist political agendas.

We can mourn the loss of a shared mythic story as another layer of "paradise lost." At the same time, we are witnessing a gradual increase in concern by everyday people in the West for those less fortunate than themselves. We also are witnessing increasingly forceful demands that Western political leaders factor compassion into their economic equations. However, we are still far from acknowledging, as many holy books say, that "our God and your God are one —there is only one shared Reality." Here we may need to put the word *God* into quotation marks for modern sensibilities and translate it as "the source and meaning of what we value in life."

The only problem with this is that the words *source* and *meaning* do not evoke any feeling in the human heart. A sense of numinous reality within, underneath and inter-penetrating everyday life, does. Perhaps humanity's future survival depends on our rediscovering the ability to feel something strange, old, awe-inspiring, and meaningful at the same time—something of more than ephemeral value. It could mean valuing what is being lost due to environmental destruction. It could lead to imagining that we are walking where Adam and Eve walked, making love where they did, circumambulating a shrine not made of stone, but revealed when we blow away the errors of ages and see the foundations of our shared human heart emerging from the dust.

NOTE

1. For instance, in the eleventh-century traditional collection *Tales of the Prophets* by Muhammad ibn Abd Allah al-Kisai, translated by W. M. Thackston, Jr. (1997).

THE ORIGINAL PILGRIMAGE

AFTER ABRAHAM AND ISHMAEL BUILD THE KAABA, ALLAH tells them:

> Call the people for pilgrimage. They will come to
> you on foot and on every kind of mount, lean from the
> journey through deep, distant mountain highways.
> (Sura 22:27)

The Arabic word for pilgrimage *(hajj)* is indirectly
related to the name of Ishmael's mother, *Hajar* (or, as we
have been spelling it in English, Hagar). Both come from
an ancient Semitic-language root that means to change
one's place, to leave, or become a "stranger." Hagar is the
one who leaves her home and becomes the mother of a new
nation. The word for pilgrimage (which has a different *h*
sound from that of Hagar) represents an action in which
"changing one's place" becomes localized around a shrine:
we turn, circle, or circumambulate in order to change our
perspective. We become strangers to our former ideas and
ideals, which we now reevaluate in the light of a larger Reality, the mysterious and sacred source of the universe.

In this sense, any real pilgrimage can be a way to let go
of concepts and theologies that do not help us become more
compassionate, loving, and surrendered people. "No god
but God" is a good theological translation of the Islamic

shahada, or "testifying to faith." "No reality but Reality" would be one that shatters whatever thought forms we have mistakenly associated with the Source of Reality itself.

Although Abraham doubts whether anyone will hear his call to pilgrimage, according to the story his voice is somehow magnified so that it reaches everyone on earth, present and future. This is reminiscent of the story told in the Quran (Sura 7:172) about the first human being. According to that story, Allah reaches into the belly of the first human and draws out all future human beings. Allah then asks them/us, *"Alastu bi-rabbikum?"*: "Am I not your Sustainer—isn't there really one teaching, one teacher, one source of food, sustenance, emotional and mental support, behind everything?" Looking at this story from an Islamic mystical perspective, Allah by this question offers humanity the opportunity to consciously fulfill the divine image, that is, to participate in the consciousness of divine unity, including an awareness of all the creatures created before us. This opportunity also includes the dubious gift of free will, the ability to both remember and forget sacred Unity. According to Sura 33, Allah offered this "job description" first to the mountains, heavens, and earth, but they all refused it. Only humanity was willing to say, *"Ba'ala sha-hidna"*—Why not? We agree to experience, live, and testify to this!

Similarly, when all beings hear Abraham's call to pilgrimage they respond, *"Labbayka allahumma labbayka!"*: "Here I am, with full heart, at your service!" This conscious willingness to be of service to the divine through service to others typifies the essential message of Islam. Groups or governments calling themselves "Islamic" would do well to measure themselves against their actual ability to be of service to all people. If theological distinctions or later legal precedents seem to stand in the way of this simple message, then it's time to consider whether these distinctions and precedents have become "partners" (in Islamic terms) with divine Unity.

On an inner level, the story of Abraham building the Kaaba and calling humanity to pilgrimage can reflect the spiritual journey of the soul. When an experience of the divine, or a deep sense of awe, awakens a deep, intuitive call to service, the foundation of our hearts is revealed. These foundations were laid before our personal birth, long ago at the mysterious outpouring of energy called the "Singularity" by scientists and the "Beginning" by mystics. Gradually, through grace and work, the spirit of guidance transforms our hearts into a shrine around which our lives revolve. According to a Sufi conception, we carry this inner Kaaba within us. When we allow our actions to circle this sacred space within us, we can never go wrong. Life becomes a process of letting go of limiting thoughts and beliefs that prevent us from being of service to the Real. Wherever we go we never feel like strangers. As the Quranic saying goes, "We come from Allah and to Allah we make our return." The coming and going happens with each breath.

If we look at a ritual of pilgrimage in relation to our everyday life, we might ask: what is the shrine or holy place around which our life, or the life of a nation, circumambulates? Is it national security, money, or consumerism? Or is there a deeper ideal still present that honors openheartedness and the possibility of fairness and a new life for those who had to leave persecution elsewhere. Wasn't the United States once a nation of Hagars? In relation to the Islamic world, couldn't the rest of us undertake an inner pilgrimage by changing our viewpoint and looking at things from the standpoint of the other? We did this during the Cold War, when many people participated in citizen diplomacy trips to the former Soviet Union and discovered that "the other" was simply ourselves with another face.

According to this part of the story, after Abraham calls humanity to pilgrimage, he makes the first pilgrimage himself, then prays: "My Sustainer, make this a city of peace and feed its people with the fruits of their work, all who believe in One Reality and in the Last Day, the day when the fruits of all actions become apparent." God responds: "Yes. And to those who deny the shared Source of Reality and cut themselves off, they will enjoy themselves for a while, but their actions will eventually lead them to the fires that purify unripe action and lead them back to the Source."

Unlike some Christian interpretations of the New Testament, the Quranic view of the afterlife does not propose any eternal damnation. There are fires of purification, but everyone comes out of the divine sauna sooner or later. All beings return to unity with Unity. Things may be uncomfortable for a while, just as they are in life, but as the Quran says, Allah is constantly forgiving and merciful:

> The animals on earth, the beings that fly on wings—
> they are all communities like you. We have omitted nothing
> from this original holy book of nature, and they shall all
> be gathered to their Nurturer and Sustainer in the end.
> (Sura 6:38)

THE SACRIFICE

Praise be to Allah, who has granted me in my old age
Ismail and Isaac. Truly my Sustainer hears all prayers.
My Sustainer, allow me and at least some of my offspring
to remain regular in prayer, and accept this prayer:
  "O Sustainer! Cover me with your forgiveness, as
well as my parents and all who believe in the support
of the One Being, on the day when the ultimate results
of all actions, the divinity in the details, become clear."
—Sura 14:39–41

In the stories of Abraham in the Quran and Islamic
tradition, the prophet continually comes across as someone figuring things out as he goes along and waiting for
the occasional divine command to clarify things. He uses
his own intelligence to understand that neither the stars,
moon, nor sun are worthy of the highest veneration. Likewise, he thinks up his trick with the idols, which, while
inspired, lands him in hot water. However, at the crucial
moment, God bails him out. Later, he has to strategize how
to get out alive when a tyrant in the area through which he's
traveling takes a fancy to Sarah. Again, his decision to dis-
semble causes some problems, and God bails him out.

  In order to keep his family line going, he ends up with
two families, one through Hagar, another through Sarah.
One could argue that he couldn't be blamed for starting a

family with Hagar, since Sarah herself felt she was past the ability to bear children and agreed to it. Nevertheless, he ends up with a challenge, and his initial response is to exile his first family, or, looked at in a more extreme way, to leave them in a desolate place and look the other way. Again, God sorts out the situation. Abraham's "saving grace," as it were, seems to be that he trusts God implicitly to do exactly the sort of rescuing that occurs. Likewise with building the Kaaba: God tells him what needs to be done, and even without knowing how to begin, he is guided step by step, or stone by stone, through the whole process, including calling all humanity to the first pilgrimage.

There is something very human about the Abraham of the Quran, which is entirely consistent with the picture of him presented in the Bible. In Islamic tradition he is called *Khalil Allah*, the "friend of the One Being." Friendship implies an intimacy not attributed to any other prophet.

We can look at all of the Islamic stories of Abraham as that of the soul's journey through life. In this sense, Abraham is the self *(nafs)* in the process of becoming a soul *(ruh)*. Through life's challenges and relationships the self becomes more fully human—a more complete reflection of the divine image created at the first Beginning. Once friendship and intimacy with our own sense of inner guidance is established, we can never go too far wrong. One does one's best and waits for the occasional moments of divinely inspired clarity. The Sufis call this dynamic the swing between *maqam*, our way of living and often blundering through everyday life, and *hal*, the moments of clear guidance from the Source. Unlike the "hero" in many great ancient stories, Abraham is not superhuman or above making mistakes. He resembles the Fool card in the Tarot, the person who goes ahead on faith, even without fully knowing what he or she is doing.

Then there's the whole matter of Abraham's willingness to sacrifice one, the other, or both of his sons. One could argue that he had already tried to sacrifice Ishmael when he dropped him and his mother in the middle of the desert. In addition, the Quran relates another story also told in the Bible: that God tests Abraham by asking him to sacrifice his son (Sura 37:100–109). In contrast to the biblical story, Abraham tells his son about the vision he has received from God and asks him his opinion. The son responds that Abraham should do as God commands him: "You will find me, if Allah so wills, a person practicing patience and perseverance!" As in the biblical account, God stops Abraham at the last minute and tells him,

> "'You have already fulfilled the vision!'" So indeed do
> We reward those who do right. For this was clearly a trial,
> and We ransomed him with a great sacrifice: And We left
> him to be remembered among future generations with this
> blessing: "Peace to Abraham!" (Sura 37:105–109)

As mentioned in my initial summary of the Islamic stories of Abraham ("The Story in Islam"), most early Quranic commentators thought this sura was referring to Isaac, who is usually named *Dhabihullah* ("sacrificed to God") in Muslim tradition. The Quran (Sura 19:54) calls Ishmael *Sadiqulwad* ("he who is true to his promise"), which could refer either to the intended sacrifice or to his willingness to help Abraham build the Kaaba.

Whoever was the intended sacrifice, Muslim, Jewish, and Christian commentators all usually draw the same lesson from the story. God tested Abraham with the ultimate test—not surrendering his own life but that of his son. Somehow this still doesn't satisfy.

We can also look at this story as describing part of the soul's journey. When the self (Abraham) has worked to bring something into manifestation (the child), then the hardest thing for the still-evolving self to do is give it up. For instance, in response to a clear inspiration or what feels like intuitive guidance, we accomplish or create something that we previously would have felt was beyond us. The tendency may be to hold on to the "fruit" of this endeavor rather than to realize and appreciate the new qualities that the process helped us develop. At some point, however, all fruit needs to fall from the tree. As in the sacrifice story, sometimes we need to let go of the outer creation, or at least be *willing* to let go, in order to continue to grow.

On the cultural level, we in the West need to look at whether we are being suffocated by the fruits of our own creativity. The many years of innovation and production have not led us to realize the spiritual side of accomplishment or creativity, that is, led us to real satisfaction in life. Rather they have trapped us in a spider's web of materialism. The excessive use of the earth's petroleum, among other things, threatens to overheat the planet. Now might be a good time to sacrifice what seems nearest and dearest, to strip back our lifestyles to what is sustainable in terms of the whole planet. Of course, this would also necessitate a sea change in our attitudes to the Middle East as well as other areas of the world that our governments see primarily as sources of raw materials to help us maintain the illusion of our own immortality a bit longer.

Some commentators feel that the stories of the attempted sacrifice in the Bible and Quran originally stem from a time ten thousand or more years ago when human sacrifice, as a strategy for survival in ancient nomadic bands, was being abandoned.[1] For millennia there had never been enough to support a large family. Life spans were short anyway and sacrifice was inevitable. Then the rise of herding and agriculture began to make such extreme sacrifices unnecessary. And yet it must have taken a leap of faith for those involved.

It is a leap of faith of the same magnitude that we face when we contemplate a world without massive armies and armories, a world where we can trust that the sort of senseless sacrifice we have taken for granted for so long is no longer necessary.

At the end of his life, Abraham asks for forgiveness for himself, for his parents (who mostly made his life more difficult), and for everyone who remembers that there is only one Source of Reality. Forgiveness is not something we need to wait to practice until the "day of the final audit." It begins whenever we stop in our tracks and begin to turn our collective lives around. It begins when we ask that our governments do the same, in the name of peace and blessings for all the children of Abraham, Sarah, and Hagar, for all the children of Adam and Eve.

NOTE

1. For instance, see Morris Berman's *Wandering God: A Study in Nomadic Spirituality* (2000).

REFERENCES FOR PART III

Ali, Yusuf A., trans. (1938). *The Holy Quran: Text, Translation, Commentary.* Lahore, India: Sh. Muhammad Ashraf.

Alim (Version 6.0), computer software, includes Quran, hadith, and other references. Silver Spring, MD: ISL Software, www.islsoftware.com

Berman, Morris. (2000). *Wandering God: A Study in Nomadic Spirituality.* Albany: State University of New York Press.

Fakhry, Majid. (2004). *An Interpretation of the Qur'an: English Translations of the Meanings (A Bilingual Edition).* New York: New York University Press.

Firestone, Reuven. (1990). *Journeys in Holy Lands: The Evolution of the Abraham-Ishmael Legends in Islamic Exegesis.* Albany: State University of New York Press.

Hixon, Lex. (2003). *The Heart of the Qur'an: An Introduction to Islamic Spirituality.* Wheaton, IL: Quest Books.

Hixon, Lex, and Fariha Al-Jerrahi. (2002). *101 Diamonds from the Oral Tradition of the Glorious Messenger Muhammad.* New York: Pir Press.

Omar, Abdul Mannan. (2003). *The Dictionary of the Holy Qur'an*. Hockessin, DE: Noor Foundation.

Thackston, Wheeler M., Jr., trans. (1997). *Tales of the Prophets (Qisas al-anbiya) by Muhammad ibn Abd Allah al-Kisai*. Chicago, IL: Kazi Publications.

EPILOGUE

From Hearing to Doing

OUR VOICES IN THIS BOOK ARE DIVERSE. WE COME OUT OF different traditions with rich and varied ways of understanding the story of the family of Abraham and draw on the thought and practices of these different religious orientations to help us connect ancient texts with our world today.

Within these pages, we suggest new liturgy; introduce new interpretations and understandings of our sacred texts; show how the teachings of our traditions rise up in the very midst of political gatherings and collisions that might seem purely "secular"; redraw the teachings that seem historically and politically attuned so as to address our inner spiritual seekings; offer suggestions for further readings in scholarly and spiritual literature; and create a new context for ourselves and each other as we gather across and beyond the lines of our three traditions.

All our traditions—Jewish, Christian, and Muslim—teach that the human race and every human being are created in the image of God. Rabbinic midrash says that when Caesar puts his image on a coin, each coin comes out identical—but that when the One who is beyond all rulers puts the divine image on the coin of every human being, each "coin" comes out unique. And the Christian Gospels teach that we can give to Caesar the coins that are Caesar's but give to God these coins of human diversity and depth that are imbued with the image of God.

Today, the various Caesars of our planet insist that we must fit into a single mold, the mold of uniformity and death. Caesars of truck bombs and hijacked airliners rage against Caesars of stealth bombers, helicopters, and artillery barrages—and the people die. The people scorch and burn, the people lose arms and legs and genitals, the people lose homes and places lovely to our God.

The pain of these deaths and of this destruction drives some of the children of Hagar, through Ishmael, and some of the children of Sarah, through Isaac, to forget that they are all children of Abraham. That we are all children of Noah and his wife, Naamah, who suffered through the danger that human violence imposes on all who dwell on our planet. That we are all children of Adam and Eve, heirs also to those forebears whose older child murdered the younger.

Through the uniqueness of our own voices, we have tried to model in this book the uniqueness of the faces that give form to the Infinite God. If we are to celebrate that God, we must in the same breath resist the idolatrous Caesars who think to impose upon us their murders. In our banks, our kindergartens, our picket lines and voting booths, as we worship in our graceful sacred buildings and in our quiet forests and on our frenzied streets, through the seasons of our joy and of our sorrow—in all these, we must remember to welcome ourselves, each other, and all who begin as strangers into the Tent that is open to all.

We need to reawaken in ourselves the "Father of Multitudes," the "Queen," the "Stranger," the "Laughing One," the "One Whom God Hears"—the voices of Abraham's family to which we have been listening in this book.

We need to rediscover in our own generation the teachings of the Polish-American rabbi Abraham Joshua Heschel, who said that "prayer is meaningless unless it is subversive, unless it seeks to overthrow and to ruin the pyramids of callousness, hatred, opportunism, falsehoods. The liturgical movement must become a revolutionary movement, seeking to overthrow the forces that continue to destroy the promise, the hope, the vision."

We need to listen to the Southern Baptist preacher Martin Luther King, Jr., who proclaimed that "we must rapidly begin the shift from a 'thing-oriented' society to a 'person-oriented' society. When machines and computers, profit motives and property rights are considered more important than people, the giant triplets of racism, materialism, and militarism are incapable of being conquered."

We must hearken to the Catholic agitator Dorothy Day, who said, "The greatest challenge of the day is: how to bring about a revolution of the heart, a revolution which has to start with each one of us?"

We must remember the Muslim teacher El Hajj Malik el-Shabazz, born Malcolm, who said, "I'm for truth, no matter who tells it. I'm for justice, no matter who it is for or against. I'm a human being first and foremost, and as such I'm for whoever and whatever benefits humanity *as a whole*."

But even more truly, more urgently, we need to re-awaken the Voice in our own voices. To tell in our own voices the stories that connect. That simply connect.

And then we must carry what we have heard into action that heals our broken family.

JOAN CHITTISTER, OSB
MURSHID SAADI SHAKUR CHISHTI
RABBI ARTHUR WASKOW

RESOURCES FOR PRACTICAL USE IN ABRAHAMIC PEACEMAKING

Introduction to the Resources

MOST OF THE RESOURCES FOR ABRAHAMIC GATHERING, prayer, study, and action that follow in this section arose from meetings of a small group of Christian, Jewish, and Muslim religious leaders and scholars who came together for long weekends in September 2004 and again in January and May 2005.

Mostly the same fifteen people, with but a few changes, took part in all these retreats. They were brought together by The Shalom Center—a network made up mostly of North American Jews, with a number of other spiritually rooted participants, that has offices in Philadelphia, Pennsylvania.

The group named itself The Tent of Abraham, Hagar, and Sarah.

The contents of this section are as follows:

- The essay by Rabbi Phyllis Berman, who facilitated most of these gatherings, on "How to Pitch Your Own Tent"—that is, on the process of those meetings;
- "The Journey Told Anew," which weaves together the Jewish/Christian and the Muslim understandings of the stories of the Abrahamic clan, and which became the spark that ignited the gatherings and this book;
- A public statement on peacemaking in the whole

Abrahamic region of the broader Near East and
Middle East;
* A call for observance in multireligious Abrahamic
ways of an unusual confluence of sacred dates and
seasons in the fall of 2005, 2006, and 2007.

One resource we have not reprinted in this book but
strongly recommend is "The Passover of Peace: A Seder
for the Children of Abraham, Hagar, and Sarah," woven by
Rabbi Arthur Waskow from traditional Passover teachings
and symbols, a previous "Seder of the Children of Abraham," Rabbi Waskow's own midrash, liturgy, prayer, and
teaching, and stories of contemporary Palestinians and Israelis in conflict and cooperation.

This Seder is built on the stories of Hagar and Sarah,
Ishmael and Isaac, rather than on the story of the Exodus
from Egypt. It has been and can be used by Jewish families,
congregations, and communities, and by groups of Jews and
Palestinians or Jews and Muslims who can together share
and rework its text.

Please visit www.beacon.org/tentofabraham for links
to the Seder and to learn more about the continuing work
of the authors of this volume on the reweaving of Abrahamic connections.

HOW TO PITCH YOUR OWN TENT

Erector-Set Directions for
Successful Interfaith Retreats

RABBI PHYLLIS BERMAN

WHEN WE COME TOGETHER, WHETHER WITH FRIENDS OR strangers, what we most want is to feel our hearts touched by one another, recognizing the humanness, actually recognizing the presence of the Other, in the other. When this happens, our time feels rich; when this doesn't happen, our time feels partly wasted.

And this is especially what we need and want when we meet with people from spiritual and religious traditions other than our own, if our meeting is grounded in seeking to see the One who is the root and the blossom of all our traditions. The image of God that appears in every human face is authentically divine precisely because each face is unique, reflecting the Infinite. So it is this uniqueness that we seek to see; in it is the One.

One aspect of that diverse uniqueness and the Unity on which we agree becomes apparent when we share our intellects. We may learn a great deal from each other, even come to understand our own selves better, by explaining to each other the thoughts and practices of our own religious path.

And we may gain from discovering how much we agree and how we differ when it come to pursuing justice, peace, the healing of the earth. These are ideas, valuable and necessary. But even this is limited, if we restrict ourselves to it.

For example: suppose that to stem the flood of violence throughout the world that has been erupting in the name of G!D, YHWH, Jesus, Allah, and all the other intimate names known to the faithful, we hope to gather leaders and teachers from the very traditions that are using violence against each other. Will it be enough to share some theories and plan some actions to reverse the cycles of violence?

Both my experience and my thought teach me that it will not be enough.

Experience first: In the summer of 2004, I took part in just such a gathering. People from all over the world— Christians, Jews, Muslims, Hindus, Buddhists, Animists— shared many ideas and projects for peace. The gathering was well facilitated. At one level, we learned a lot. But ultimately, we returned home a week later not having been deeply touched by one another. I felt no deep need to keep in touch with the brilliant, creative, generous people I had met.

This felt truly shocking. And saddening.

At the level of thought and ideas, how can we account for that result? The Jewish mystics teach us that there are four worlds of reality: *asiya* (the physical world of action); *yetzira* (the emotional world of feelings); *briyya* (the intellectual world of ideas); and *atzilut* (the soul world of Oneness). The deeper task of meeting in an interfaith community is the sharing of our lives in all four worlds, not only the world of intellect.

When we planned the first gatherings of the group that was to become the Tent of Abraham, Hagar, and Sarah, we knew in our minds and hearts that what we wanted from the experience of these gatherings was not only a plan of action and an increased intellectual understanding of one another but also a real sense of knowing and caring about one another as fellow human beings created in G!D's (whatever Her name) image.

We began the first gathering by inviting all those present to share, briefly, with the whole group, just a single story from their spiritual journey—specifically, a moment that we recognized as having brought us to this peacemaking point in our lives. What deep experience in our own lives, for example, had brought each of us to want to connect with other traditions?

From that powerful beginning, it was possible for us to pray together (not just observe one another in prayer) in ways that were authentic to and respectful of one another's traditions.

One Jewish participant led a service by using chant and meditation rooted in Jewish prayer, rather than the flood of Hebrew words that usually make up a communal Jewish service. Chanting these far fewer words, transliterated into English letters and translated, was a way to invite everyone to understand, participate, and take the meaning deep within.

A Christian noted how important food and eating are for all of our traditions. He pointed out that the Mass—the peak moment of "prayerful eating" in Christianity—was not appropriate for an interfaith gathering, but that eating together in an "agape meal" was an authentic New Testament practice not limited to Christians alone and that such a meal could be an act of prayer.

Another used what we might have thought the hardest, hottest of frameworks—the Last Supper—as a way to get inside the skins of the different kinds of people at the table, then and now. She invited us to take on one or another of the personae as the Gospels describe them, and thus to express the hopes, fears, angers, and doubts of different people facing what might or might not be a spiritual transformation.

The Muslims invited us to read some Sufi poetry, to chant the names of God, and to dance in the rhythmic forms of *zikr*, authentic Muslim spiritual practices, though different from the classical five-times-a-day prayer.

Getting to know one another's hearts did not prevent us from accomplishing the task of formulating ways to work together toward peace as the children of Abraham, Hagar, and Sarah. If anything, it deepened our resolve to complete the task, because we had come to care about one another. We had personalized the faces of the other, even in the short time we were together.

So we developed a public appeal for changes in U.S. governmental policy toward peacemaking in the broader Middle East, in the regions where Abraham traveled—from Babylonia (Iraq) to Canaan (Israel and Palestine) to Egypt to the Kaaba (Saudi Arabia).

And precisely because we were from different communities, used to our own different sacred calendars, we discovered an astonishing confluence of sacred times in 2005, 2006, and 2007. First we realized the unusual confluence of the sacred Jewish and Muslim months of Tishrei and Ramadan, and then the confluence with them of the Protestant and Orthodox Christian observance of Worldwide Communion Sunday and of the feast day of St. Francis of Assisi. Out of these discoveries arose a whole plan for multireligious observance of this holy season.

And as part of the decision making about these projects, individuals among us agreed to take on specific tasks to make the projects real.

In planning interfaith events, this is our strong recommendation: Each event must incorporate aspects of the four worlds:

- Opportunities to know the soul journeys of people whose paths may have been parallel to ours;
- Opportunities to celebrate the One through the specific idioms of one another's religions;
- Opportunities to understand the ways in which our traditions are similar and different in philosophy, theology, and practice;
- Opportunities to plan actions together that keep our Abrahamic families in peaceful connection with one another.
- Opportunities to eat, dance, and move together.

We were deliberately beginning with the Abrahamic communities, while at the same time intending to build the open tent that, according to tradition, Abraham's family built—a tent open in all four directions so that people coming from everywhere and anywhere might be nourished.

Our experience may be helpful for any effort at making interfaith connection at a deep level.

So here are our suggestions for shaping a successful interfaith retreat encounter:

1. Invite a small number of people (12–24), being sure to balance the number of Jews, Christians, and Muslims. But keep in mind this may not mean mechanical numerical equality: There are many more Christians than Muslims or Jews in American society. Yet be sure to have enough Jews and Muslims so that they will not feel awkwardly lonely, or like tokens.
2. Seek also a balance in terms of gender, age, race, and color.
3. Make people's attendance conditional on their ability and willingness to come on time at the start of the retreat and remain until the end. No exceptions—this is essential!

4. After welcoming people, ask everyone to introduce themselves by sharing one story from the spiritual journey that called them into this interfaith gathering. Set an allotted time frame (10–15 minutes each). Depending on the number of people, you may have to allocate several sessions to incorporate all the stories; use wordless melodies and/or silence after each story or every few stories so that people can digest what they've heard.

5. Incorporate aspects of communal prayer—Muslim, Jewish, Christian—that individuals can lead and the group can share, not as observers but as participants. This means choosing prayers, practices, and languages that are accessible to the group and that everyone can do without being disrespectful to their own religion. Leave time as well for whatever more distinctive "members-only prayer" may be necessary.

6. Intersperse business and action meetings with prayer sessions, story-sharing sessions, meals together, some form of dance or movement, and informal time so that the balance between body, heart, mind, and soul is maintained.

7. At the final session, leave time not only for a summary of the action directives that have emerged from the meetings, but for people to give feedback to organizers and one another about their experiences with one another at this gathering.

Rabbi Phyllis Berman was guide and facilitator for many of the sessions of the Tent of Abraham, Hagar, and Sarah. She is the founder (1979) and director of the Riverside Language Program, an intensive school in New York City for adult immigrants and refugees from all over the world. From 1993 to 2003 she was director of the summer program of the Elat Chayyim retreat center, and she is the coauthor of A Time for Every Purpose Under Heaven: The Jewish Life-Spiral as a Spiritual Journey.

THE JOURNEY TOLD ANEW

Rabbi Arthur Waskow and
Murshid Saadi Shakur Chishti

The whole enterprise of this book and the creation of the group of Jews, Christians, and Muslims that became the Tent of Abraham, Hagar, and Sarah began when the two of us wrote this poetic narrative and sought to grow it into life beyond the written word as well. We owe special thanks to Pecki Witonsky of Philadelphia for bringing the two of us together to do this.

We wrote it to unify the Jewish/Christian and Muslim narratives of the Abrahamic saga without negating the uniqueness of either version of the family story. We have made clear the places in which the tales and memories diverge, while providing a coherent narrative that affirms the many places where they track each other. We have in mind that some communities might use this new telling of the story, either in actually meeting with each other or in learning how to hear each other's wisdoms.

That One Who brings being itself into being,
that One for Whom all time, all space, is ever-present,
that One Who is the Breath of Life,
Who breathes compassion,
YHWH/Allah/God,
called Abram to go forward with his family,

going outward for the sake of going inward,
to leave the broken place of shattered truth
and seek a wholeness that God would let him see.

He looked for this wholeness in the stars and moon,
but when they set, he said,
"I love not those who set."
He looked for wholeness in the sun, rising in its
    splendor,
but when the sun had set, he said,
"I am finished now mistaking anything for the One,
I turn my face toward the One who created heaven and
    earth."

He argued with his father and community,
preached the One and broke their idols,
challenging any image of clay to speak in retort.
His people tried to burn him, but the One preserved
    him.
He walked through the fire toward a new life,
leaving the outer land of his ancestry,
leaving the inner land of shadows and confused reflections
that kept him from the One.

He went.
And with him went both wholeness and division.
Two families that were a single family he birthed.
Two eyes to see that gave reality a depth
no single eye, no single "I," could see.

Two stories that together help us see and hear a deeper
    truth.

From God Abram received the added *hei* of conscious
    breath: Abraham,

and Sarah/Queen—and Hagar/Stranger—
to bring forth two families, two stories
that have these four millennia sought reconnection.

The Stranger's son yearned long before his birth for God's
    protection
and received the Blessing—"God Will Hear": The name
    Yishmael.
Wild shall you live in the wilderness,
your hand and the hand of all upraised,
and you shall come to live, to see, your brothers face to
    face.

And Sarah's son came laughing through the Gate of
    Doubt,
His forebears laughing to hear the prophecy that,
old and withered, they might still beget and birth.
So when delight poured over them
they laughed again with pleasure and with joy,
and named their newborn Yitzhak, Laughing One.

According to the story that the clan of Yitzhak tells,
Yishmael also laughed.
And Sarah felt that the laughter of her son
could not live face to face with the laughter of the
    Stranger's son.
So Sarah persuaded Abraham to send Hagar and Ishmael
    into the wilderness.

When they arrived, Hagar said to Abraham,
"Do you leave us with no water and food?"
No answer.
"Is the One telling you to do this?"
"Yes," he said.
"Then I am satisfied to remain in the arms of the Holy
    One."

As her water ran out, her child was dying.
Hagar ran back and forth between two hills seven times,
looking for anyone who would help.
Finally she saw Gabriel, digging out a spring with his heel,
the well of Zamzam in one story,
the Well of the Living One Who Sees Me in another.

Gabriel said,
"Don't be afraid. The One never neglects the people of the
    One."
Look for help outside, but expect it always
under your own feet, springing from the grace
of Sacred Unity.

Another tribe saw a bird circling that well,
just like the wings of freedom circle
new inspiration from the One
gushing from within the soul.
Drawn by the well, more people came,
formed a community, opened a future
for Hagar and Ishmael.

And in the story remembered by the folk of Yitzhak:
When God hearkened to their outcry,
echoing the name of Ishmael in listening compassion,
God's open ears opened their eyes to see—
And so the well they saw was
The Well of the Living One Who Sees Me.
And so God blessed their future.

The folk of Yitzhak also teach that in a twin journey of
    great danger,
Abraham took Yitzhak, his son with queenly Sarah,
with him on a journey to be offered up.
When God saw him bound upon an awesome rock,

God sent a messenger to clarify:
This offering must lead to life, not death.
Abraham lifted his eyes and saw a ram to take the place of
    Laughter,
And Isaac laughed to see the transformation.
Abraham named the place the "Mount of Seeing,"
where "God will see."

Later, Abraham and Hagar,
now known as Keturah/Sweetly Spiced,
reconnected and lived joyfully together.
And as the memories of the children of Ishmael teach,
It was at the Kaaba that Ishmael
willingly surrendered to God's will
when Abraham was preparing to make of him an offering.
But God did not desire his death,
and Ishmael lived to give birth to the Arab peoples,
and to the tradition that was fulfilled with Muhammad,
on whom be peace.

Together Abraham and Ishmael built the first temple at
    Mecca.
They sang the praises of the Holy One,
placing the holy sound and name
into each stone as they lifted one upon another.
After finishing, they prostrated and walked around the
    Kaaba,
allowing the divine breath of the One to
infuse each movement, each footstep.

"O Sacred Unity, to whom alone we bow,"
said Abraham,
"Make this a city of peace,
feed all of its people with
the fruits of your grace.

Accept our service,
for you only hear through all ears.
You are the Knower behind all
knowing and all knowledge."

Full of years and filled with sacred wisdom,
Abraham died.
Isaac and Ishmael came together
to mourn and bury the one whose dangers they had dared,
the one whose unity they had unfolded,
and to live together at the Well of the Living One Who
    Sees Me.

THE TENT OF ABRAHAM, HAGAR, AND SARAH

A Call for Peacemaking

This call, springing from spiritual and religious concerns, couched in religious language, and addressing urgent issues of public policy, came forth from the earliest meeting of the Tent of Abraham, Hagar, and Sarah. It was endorsed by a number of national religious leaders; in order to reach as wide an audience as possible, it was published as a full-page ad in the New York Times *of January 14, 2005; and it was ultimately signed by more than one thousand people of faith.*

Among the initiating signers (all signing as individuals; organizations are noted for identification only) were Rev. Bob Edgar, general secretary of the National Council of Churches; Dr. Sayyid Muhammad Syeed, general secretary of the Islamic Society of North America; Joan Chittister, OSB, former president of the Society of Women Religious of America; Jim Wallis, Sojourners; Imam Abdul Feisal Rauf; Saadi Shakur Chishti/ Neil Douglas-Klotz; Imam Talib Abdur Rashid; Meena Sharify-Funk; Dr. Susannah Heschel; and Rabbis Rachel Cowan, Elliot Dorff, Amy Eilberg, Zalman Schachter-Shalomi, Gerry Serotta, David Teutsch, Arthur Waskow, and Sheila Weinberg.

We offer it here both as a substantive example of proposals grounded in shared interfaith concerns aimed at shaping public policy in a difficult area—peace in the broader Middle East—and as an example of how a small group of committed people of the Abrahamic faiths can reach out to established leaders and to the larger public.

We are members of the families of Abraham—Muslims, Christians, Jews.

Our traditions teach us to have compassion, seek justice, and pursue peace for all peoples. We bear especially deep concern for the region where Abraham grew and learned, taught and flourished. Today that region stretches from Iraq, where Abraham grew up, to Israel and Palestine, where he sojourned, and to Mecca and Egypt, where he visited.

Today our hearts are broken by the violence poured out upon the peoples of that broad region.

That violence has included terrorist attacks on and kidnappings of Americans, Israelis, Iraqis, Europeans, and others by various Palestinian and Iraqi groups and by Al Qaeda; the occupation of Palestinian lands by Israel and of Iraq by the United States; and the torture of prisoners by several different police forces, military forces, and governments in the region.

From our heartbreak at these destructive actions, we intend to open our hearts more fully to each other and to the suffering of all peoples.

In the name of the One God Whom we all serve and celebrate, we condemn all these forms of violence. To end the present wars and to take serious steps toward the peace that all our traditions demand of us, we call on governments and on the leaders of all religious and cultural communities to act.

We urge the U.S. government to set a firm and speedy date for completing the safe return home from Iraq of all American soldiers and civilians under military contract. We urge the UN to work directly with Iraqi political groupings to transfer power in Iraq to an elected government.

We urge the UN, the U.S., the European Union, and Russia to convene a comprehensive peace conference through which the governments of Israel, the Palestinian Authority, Iran, and all Arab states conclude a full diplomatic, economic, and cultural peace with Israel and Palestine, defined approximately on the 1967 boundaries, with small mutual adjustments.

We urge the international community to work out lawful and effective means to deal with the dangers of international terrorism, the spread of nuclear and similar weapons, and conflicts over the control of oil and water.

We ourselves will act to create transnational and interfaith networks of Jews, Christians, and Muslims who will covenant together
—to insist that governments take these steps,
—to undertake whatever nonviolent actions are necessary to prevent more violence and achieve a just peace throughout the region,
—and to grow grassroots relationships that bind together those who have been enemies into a Compassionate Coalition.

According to tradition, Abraham kept his tent open in all four directions, the more easily to share his food and water with travelers from anywhere. In that spirit, we welcome all those who thirst and hunger for justice, peace, and dignity to join in affirming this statement.

THE SACRED SEASON OF
ABRAHAMIC SACRED SEASONS

*This statement was initiated by the group of Jews, Christians,
and Muslims who gathered in several retreats as the Tent of
Abraham, Hagar, and Sarah. It was then, in mid-2005, adopted
by a number of major national religious organizations. (See a
partial list at its end.) We are offering it as both a useful practical proposal for how to address the continuing confluence of the
Abrahamic sacred seasons, and as a way to think about shaping
sacred connections with each other. For a brief review of the calendar connections, see the note at the end of this essay.*

At a moment of increasing religious war, violence, and re-
pression, God has given our spiritual and religious traditions a gift of time:

During the fall of 2005, 2006, and 2007, an unusual
confluence of sacred moments in the different Abrahamic
traditions invites us to pray with or alongside each other,
share food and stories, and work together for peace, justice,
human rights, and the healing of our wounded earth.

The sacred Muslim lunar month of Ramadan and the
sacred Jewish lunar month of Tishrei, which includes the
High Holy Days and Sukkot, both begin at the same time
in these three years. And there is more: October 4 is the
Feast of St. Francis of Assisi (who almost alone of all Christian leaders of his generation opposed the Crusades and
studied with Islamic teachers, as well as connecting deeply

with all the creatures of the earth); the first Sunday in October is Worldwide (Protestant/Orthodox) Communion Sunday.

There is much that we could do to heal the world during this sacred season made up of sacred times:

Most powerfully, perhaps, from sunrise to sunset on the day that for Muslims is one of the fast days of Ramadan and for Jews is the fast day of Yom Kippur, Christians and indeed all Americans could also observe a Fast for Reflection, Repentance, Reconciliation, and Renewal.

All of us could learn from the passage of Isaiah that in Jewish tradition is read on Yom Kippur morning. God, speaking through Isaiah, says, "Do you think the fast that I demand this day is to bow down your head like a bulrush? No! The fast I demand is that you feed the poor, house the homeless, clothe the naked, and break off the handcuffs on your prisoners."

So for our generation, this fast could be dedicated to serving God not through prayer alone but also by making a commitment that later in the sacred month, we will undertake some action in which the different communities together embody God's commands to *seek peace, feed the poor, heal the earth.*

Other possibilities for action:

- Churches could invite other congregations to join in learning about, celebrating, and acting on the teachings of Francis of Assisi.
- Jews could invite others into the sukkah, a leafy hut that is open to the wind and rain. Traditionally, "sacred guests" are invited in, and, according to the teachings of the ancient rabbis, blessings are invoked upon "the seventy nations" of the world during Sukkot. Traditional prayers implore God to

"spread the sukkah of shalom" over us. These are perfect rubrics for peacemaking among the children of Abraham and all humanity with each other and with all the earth.

• Muslims could host Iftar—a break-fast meal—for other communities, after nightfall on any of the evenings of Ramadan. And they could invite others to join in celebrating some aspects of Eid el-Fitr (the feast at the end of Ramadan), and Jews and Christians could (as Jews have done for centuries in Morocco) bring food to that celebration.

• Synagogues could set aside a time during Yom Kippur or the Shabbat just before, or at another special time during the month, to read and discuss with Muslims the Torah's story (Gen. 25:7–11) of the joining of Isaac and Ishmael to bury their father Abraham, and then to achieve reconciliation at the Well of the Living One Who Sees Me.

Can imams at the festival time of Eid al-Adha, which commemorates the offering-up of Ishmael, invite Jews to tell the other family story, of Isaac's ordeal?

Can rabbis, leading the celebration of Rosh Hashanah when Jews read the story of Ishmael's expulsion and of Isaac's offering up, invite Muslims to teach about the offering-up of Ishmael?

Jewish tradition teaches that the ram's horn—blown in the midst of hearing the Abrahamic stories on Rosh Hashanah—echoes the ram that Abraham offered up in replacement of his son; and that the sobbing sounds of blowing the shofar echo the sobs of an enemy of Israel as she fears her son, the Canaanite Sisera, has fallen in battle. Can Muslims and Christians draw on this compassionate understanding of the ram's horn?

Muslim tradition teaches that when Abraham heard

God commanding him to slay not his son but a sheep, he gave the meat of the sheep to the poor and hungry—and set a precedent for such sharing every year when Muslims remember the moment. Can Jews and Christians learn from that understanding of an offering?

Our communities could together take some action during the month to protect human rights, heal the earth, and seek peace in the whole region where Abraham, Hagar, and Sarah sojourned.

A call to all Americans to join in a nationwide fast, and to create shared multireligious local and regional events during the month, has been endorsed by the National Council of Churches; the Islamic Society of North America; Pax Christi; the Fellowship of Reconciliation; ALEPH: Alliance for Jewish Renewal and its rabbinic affilate, Ohalah; the Jewish Committee for Isaiah's Vision (an ad hoc committee made up of more than one hundred rabbis and other Jewish leaders), and a number of local and regional groups.

In 2006 and 2007, Tishrei, Ramadan, and the Feast of St. Francis will again coincide. With three successive years' experience of making sacred connection, perhaps we can learn to continue even when the calendar is not so filled with God's surprise.

Both Jewish and Muslim calendars are rooted in lunar "months." The Jewish calendar, however, inserts (seven times in every nineteen years) an additional entire lunar month, to make the various months stay in the same season of the solar year. Thus the month of Nisan, containing Passover and considered the first of the months, comes always in the spring. Tishrei, seen as the seventh month by counting from Nisan in the spring, and containing Rosh Hashanah, Yom Kippur, Sukkot, and Shmini Atzeret/Simchat Torah, comes always in the fall. It is the sabbatical month, filled with holy festivals at every phase of the moon.

The Muslim calendar ignores the solar year, so that the lunar months proceed in a stately dance through the solar year. For this reason, Ramadan, the month in which the Quran was revealed and the most holy month in the Muslim year, coincides with the most holy Jewish month only for two or three years at a time, once in every generation. After 2007, it will be another thirty-some years before Ramadan and Tishrei coincide.

Both months begin with the new moon. Jewish tradition has accepted astronomers' advance calculations of the day on which this falls; Muslim tradition requires an actual sighting of the sliver of new moon. So sometimes the dates are a day or two apart. In 2006, Rosh Hashanah begins on the night of Friday, September 22; in 2007, on September 12. Ramadan will begin with the actual sighting of the new moon, within a day or so of those dates.

October 4 each year is the feast day of St. Francis of Assisi. The first Sunday of October is Worldwide Communion Sunday for Protestant and Orthodox Christians. Thus in 2006 and 2007, both these dates will fall within Ramadan and Tishrei.

WHY HAGAR LEFT

Rabbi Phyllis Berman

*In some ways, this story follows in the tradition of Jewish midrash
on the Torah text. But it is an unusual and radical midrash: even
while it reports and takes into account all the Torah's tales and
hints about the Hagar-Sarah relationship and other aspects of
Sarah's and Hagar's lives, it understands the Torah's description
of the relationship between Hagar and Sarah as a fictive story
created by the two women and told by Sarah to Abraham in order
to explain and justify Hagar's need to leave the family along with
Ishmael.*

*By reframing the Torah story in this way, this tale—evi-
dently inherited from generations of women who claim to have
been told the real story of Hagar's and Sarah's relationship—may
be seen to stand beyond both the Jewish/Christian and the Muslim versions of the Abrahamic saga. It affirms a warm relationship, rather than conflict or distance, between the mothers of both
communities and traditions. So it may arise out of a submerged
strand of the Jewish midrashic tradition, but it walks forth beyond a specifically Jewish, or Christian, or Muslim perspective.*

*For these reasons we thought it belonged in none of the three
sections of this book that speak specifically from these perspectives,
but separately, as a resource for women—and for men—who want
to explore new territory. To use the feminine verb and pronoun*

forms of the Hebrew phrase that sent Abraham on his journey:
L'chi lach — "Go forth beyond yourself to explore your deepest in-
most self."

One day when I was sixteen, I came home from school
very upset. My mother asked me what was wrong. I told her
that Danny, the love of my life, was spending a lot of time
with my second-best friend, Tamar. And I was frightened.
I could only see Danny on weekends because he went to a
different high school; but Tamar got to see him all the time
—at school and at their synagogue's youth group.

At the moment they were only friends, but I knew that
Tamar really liked Danny, and I knew that he was also interested in her.

"So you're jealous of her?" said my mother.

"Well, of course," I said. "What else can I feel? I'm
worried I'll lose him; in fact, I'll lose them both."

"Where did you get the idea that two women have to
compete over a man?" my mother asked with a sparkle in
her eyes.

Incredulously, I blurted out, "Come on! From the time
I was an infant, I've gone to *shul*; from the time I started
Hebrew school, I've read the Torah. We hear the story of
the competition between Sarah and Hagar not just once but
twice a year in the Torah reading cycle. It's all about jealousy over Abraham's affection! How can you ask me that
question so innocently? I've been taught jealousy and competition from my birth."

"And from your birth," my mother said, patting the
chair beside her to invite me to sit down, "I've been waiting
to have this conversation with you. But I had to wait till you
were ready—more than ready. So at last it's time; at last it's
clear you need to hear what I'm about to say.

"The Torah you've been learning—it's not the whole
story. How do I know? My mother told me when I was

about your age; she had heard it from her mother, who had heard it from her mother, all the way back through all the generations. What she told me is the *real* story of Sarah and Hagar..."

Sarai and her boyfriend, Abram—those were their names until late in their lives—grew up in the same little town. Not only were they cousins, they were friends from childhood. So it was no surprise to anyone when their friendship turned to love.

Most of the young folks they knew stayed close to home, even when the time had come to marry. But Abram and Sarai were different. Sarai heard the words over and over, as if in a dream: *L'chi lach*—leave *where* you are, to learn *who* you are.

So she and Abram left their families and their hometown and all that was familiar to them, to make their new life together.

As they journeyed, they came to a town where a powerful pharaoh was in charge. At first it seemed a good place to live, because land was plentiful for grazing cattle and growing crops. But Sarai and Abram quickly noticed that, while there were some men in the area, there were no other women to be seen.

Abram made some discreet inquiries and learned that all of the town's women were living under the pharaoh's "protection" in his palace. Even worse—in the past, some men had protested when the pharaoh's officers had come to take the women to the palace. Those men had simply disappeared. The whisper was that they were most likely dead.

"We should never have left home!" Abram thought. Night after night, he woke up trembling: Pharaoh might kill him too, in order to add Sarai to his conquests.

So one morning Abram said to Sarai, "If Pharaoh asks us, we'll tell him you're my sister."

"I suppose it's almost true," said Sarai. "You are my cousin. And I love that song you used to sing to me—'How sweet is your love, my sister, my bride!'" She looked into his frightened face. "All right; I'm willing."

Sure enough, not long after that the pharaoh asked about them. Learning they were siblings, he ordered Sarai into his harem. As you can imagine, Sarai was terrified: she was separated from her beloved Abram and didn't know what was going to happen to her. So she looked around for a friend and quickly found another young woman, who only weeks before had herself been added to the collection of Pharaoh's women. And she was a foreigner too, from a distant city—so far away that the other women called her "Hagar" (the Stranger).

So Sarai and Hagar, both far from home, uncertain when they'd be released or what would happen until then, both new to the palace culture, became immediate and intimate friends.

Now when the pharaoh had first approached Abram and Sarai, he had promised that she'd be free of her palace duties and able to return to Abram's home after a year. And so he promised all the women before they entered his palace. But when Sarai and Hagar looked around, they could see women of all ages. It looked to them as though women were remaining in the harem far longer than a single year.

When they asked the other women how long they had lived in the palace, they heard the same story over and over again. Yes, the pharaoh had said they might leave after a year, but by that time each of them had borne a child. The pharaoh told them they could leave if they wanted to; but the child, his child, must remain in the palace. What woman, each one said in her own way, could walk away from a child still nursing at the breast? So the single year of servitude turned into many years, the child into children, and after a while they could no longer extricate themselves from the pharaoh's home.

The key to freedom, Sarai and Hagar said to each other, is not to become pregnant during this year. But how could they avoid it when none of the other women had been able to? They thought and thought, they talked and talked. And finally they remembered that, in their own hometowns, there had been a special feast at the sighting of the new moon each month. In the women's community where Sarai came from, it was called "Rosh Chodesh." The women talked through the night, one idea melting into another until they had the perfect plan.

The next day the two women gained an audience with Pharaoh, who was delighted to receive the newest additions to his harem. They told him how it was the custom in their traditions to celebrate the new moon: he should invite all the men in his retinue to a monthly feast, which would be prepared, not by the royal cooks and bakers, but by the women. The pharaoh so much liked the idea of a monthly gathering of men to eat and drink that he hardly thought twice when the women mentioned that once the food and wine were prepared, the women would go off into the woods by themselves for a night or two, to celebrate the moon's fecundity.

"Ah, but that night or two were crucial!" my mother said. "When you live with other women in a college dormitory, you'll see. For when many women live together, they often begin to menstruate on the same cycle. And in those days when there were no electric lights, women's cycles, like the tides, mirrored the rhythms of the moon as it waxed and waned each month. Those days of the new moon—that was when the women were most fertile!"

Sarai and Hagar knew that if the women were out of the palace and away from Pharaoh during the most fertile point of their month, they would probably not get pregnant. And for some months, the plan worked very well indeed. None of the women got pregnant—and Pharaoh didn't even notice. That was because there were still women who had already become pregnant before the New Moon celebrations started. They kept having babies. Pharaoh and his men reveled in the feasts, eating and drinking the finest of the women's dishes.

For Sarai and Hagar, the months passed joyfully, each new moon another step toward their day of freedom. Each month, they felt safer from a lifetime sentence.

Four months, five months, six months—and then Pharaoh realized something strange was happening. No morning sickness, no bellies swelling. What had happened to halt all fertility?

And then one afternoon, when Abram made his weekly visit into the ruler's gardens where he could talk and walk with his "sister" Sarai, Pharaoh just happened to be standing on his balcony.

Sarai and Abram were deep in conversation. Now, you know how it is when two people love each other—how they look at one another, how they touch. Even from the distance of his balcony, the pharaoh could see in the energy field of their loving glance that this was not the look one would expect between a brother and a sister. He began to think about life in his palace in the recent months, and suddenly all the different pieces of information fell into place. He ordered Abram and Sarai into his presence immediately.

"You lied to me," the pharaoh roared. "Anyone can see you are husband and wife, not brother and sister."

"In our tradition," Abram said, "it is common to refer to our brides as our sisters. This is merely a misunderstanding," he assured the pharaoh. "Even our poetry..."

"Poetry, shmoetry! You have bewitched my kingdom with your trickery!" said Pharaoh. "I have been cursed with infertility since you have come here. Get out of my palace and away from my lands this instant, and let us return to our blessed state of birthing many babies."

Abram was ready to leave immediately, but Sarai balked. "I'm not leaving here without my dear friend Hagar," she said determinedly, looking Pharaoh in the eye.

"You are lucky to get out of here with your lives," Pharaoh fumed. "Take Hagar," he said. "Just get yourselves out of here and leave us in peace."

And that is how it happened that the companions Sarai and Hagar and the couple Sarai and Abram became a family of three. It was no surprise that just as Sarai loved both Abram and Hagar, so Abram and Hagar came to love one another as well. The three settled in Hebron and peacefully went on with their lives.

Well—*mostly* peacefully, because for several years neither Sarai nor Hagar became pregnant. "Maybe our trick has brought a curse on both of us?" They worried. They prayed together: "You who are the source of all life and all liberty, You who heard our prayers for freedom from the pharaoh's palace, hear our prayers for new life now."

So it was an enormous relief when Hagar's belly did begin to swell. When the son of Hagar and Abram was born, the three called him Ishmael—"God hears"—for God had listened to their prayers. If you've seen how dear friends or close family members delight in the births of one another's children, so it was with Sarai, who adored Ishmael as fully as Hagar and Abram did. There's more than enough work for two mothers when a newborn comes into a family, and Sarai was involved with Ishmael's parenting in every way but one.

The one thing that Sarai could not do was nurse the baby, and, according to my mother, when Sarai watched Hagar soothe and satisfy the baby at her breast, it caused her grief. She yearned for a baby born from her own body, but in all other ways she loved Ishmael as her own.

The household flourished; living together was easy. And the years passed. Sarai had almost made her peace with the fact that her body would bear no children when their household was visited by three strange-seeming guests. First the three suggested that both Sarai and Abram slow down and breathe more. They even urged them both to add a breathing sound to their names as a reminder: "Sarahhh" and "Avrahham." And if they were to do that, the visitors predicted, within the year Sarai herself would give birth to a son.

Sarai laughed to hear such news. "After all these years?" she said—in a mixture of joy and disbelief. Yet, filled with hope, she and Abram agreed to rename themselves as the visitors had suggested: Sarah and Abraham.

Now you may think that everything was finally perfect, but I'm sorry to say that a strange shadow fell upon the family right before the birth of Sarah's baby. Abraham awoke one morning full of dreams about a commanding, transcendent, lordly God. In his dreams he had heard this God demand the circumcision of all the males in the family—the adolescent Ishmael, the aging Abraham, and all future newborn boys—to hallow the male genitals to create life for ongoing generations.

Abraham told these words to Sarah and Hagar, and the women were outraged. "You mean to say that you want to take our Ishmael—a thirteen-year-old just coming to terms with his body's change from boyhood to manhood—and cut off the skin at the tip of his penis?" Hagar said incredulously.

"Yes," Abraham answered. "I, and all the men of our clan and our village, and all the boy children, including our Ishmael, must be circumcised.

"For God insists that on the eighth day of life we will circumcise newborns, but now we must consecrate men and boys of all ages so that our people will be as numerous as grains of sand on the seashore or stars in the sky."

The women looked at each other in disbelief. They could barely tolerate the thought of maiming male children, let alone the men in the community. It made no sense, they thought; and yet Abraham was so certain that it was what God wanted. Finally and reluctantly, they agreed, and the circumcisions were done.

But from that moment on, a gulf opened between the two women and Abraham. If he could dream such weird dreams, such dangerous and outrageous dreams, who knew what might be next?

And yet all this was put aside when Sarah delivered a healthy baby boy. To this son the three of them gave the name Isaac—"Laughing One"—because the news of his coming had caused all of them to laugh with delight.

The family of five continued to grow in love and prosperity, until one morning Sarah awoke from a terrible dream. She was so distressed that she told it to Hagar: In her nightmare, Abraham had had another dream. This time God had told him to take his firstborn son to a nearby mountain and, like so many of their neighbors, who believed that sacrificing living beings insured continued fertility, sacrifice him. As Sarah told of the dream, she began to cry. Her body shook and her voice broke.

Hagar put her arms around Sarah. "Beloved Sarah, it is just a dream," said Hagar.

"Beloved Hagar, it is just a dream," said Sarah.

"It is just a dream of a dream," said each woman to the other.

But the dream came to Sarah once again, and then once more. "Three times!" she said to Hagar. "It will no longer leave me in the morning. Remember when Abraham dreamed that God wanted our oldest son circumcised? Is it so impossible that he might dream that God wants him to sacrifice our oldest son?"

Sarah and Hagar didn't know what to think; since the circumcision, they were not so confident about Abraham and the voices he chose to listen to. "What can we do if Abraham decides to take our Ishmael to sacrifice him?" they cried. And so they sat and talked and planned and plotted through the day and into the night, just as they had done so many years before, in the pharaoh's palace.

And once again, they agreed on an idea, this time to protect Ishmael from Abraham's potential dream. The plan is one we know well: it's the one we read about in the Torah. If Sarah were to tell Abraham this preposterous story about Ishmael teasing Isaac and demand that Abraham send Ishmael and Hagar away from the household, he would have to believe her, because he knew without a doubt how bound together the women and the boys had been. So he would send Hagar and Ishmael away.

It was a terrible plan, a heartbreaking one, but one that would keep Ishmael alive and out of Abraham's reach.

We all know what happened: Sarah did tell Abraham that she and Isaac could no longer stand to live with Hagar and Ishmael. Abraham couldn't understand it, but Sarah was so insistent that Abraham agreed, with a heavy heart, to send them away.

The night before Hagar and Ishmael were to go, the two women sat up, alternately weeping and reminiscing, and, each in her own hand, they filled two scrolls with writing. In each was the real story of their love and friendship through all the years they had lived together. Hagar placed her scroll in Sarah's hands, to give to a daughter-in-law or other female relative. Sarah put her parchment in Hagar's hands for the same purpose.

So it was that Hagar and Ishmael left the household and

went out into the desert. How they survived there and made a life for themselves is a story for another day. It's enough to say that they lived a good and long life. Ishmael had many children and won a great deal of respect among those with whom he settled.

Sarah was never the same after Hagar and Ishmael went their own way. She became withdrawn and lonely, barely consoling herself with mothering the growing Isaac. Although she believed that her deception had saved Ishmael's life, it had taken from her most of her own life energy.

You can imagine, then, how shocked, how outraged she was many years later when, indeed, Abraham did have the dream she had seen in her own vision. For in his dream, Abraham did hear God commanding him to take his son, his only son, his beloved son, Isaac, up to Mount Moriah and to sacrifice him there. Abraham did take Isaac and was ready to sacrifice him on that day. But at the last moment, God sent a ram to take Isaac's place on the altar.

When Abraham and Isaac returned home after this terrifying journey, Sarah was on her deathbed, grief-stricken once more and half-crazed that everyone she had ever loved would be lost to her. When she saw that Isaac had returned, miraculously alive, she blessed him and gave him the parchment that Hagar had written.

"This scroll," Sarah said, "is my gift to your wife if you should marry. I don't expect to live long enough to give it to her myself, but there is a story she and her offspring must know."

So it was, my mother told me, that Isaac presented Rebekah with this mysterious gift from his mother, Sarah; Rebekah eventually gave it to her daughter-in-law Leah, who gave it to her daughter Dina, and so it passed from generation to generation through the ages. When the actual scrolls disappeared, women just told the story to their daughters and granddaughters, to their nieces and their cousins.

Through this whole story, my mother and I had been sitting side by side. Her gaze had been turned inward, toward the past, more than at me. But now she took my arm and turned the two of us to face each other. And then she said, "At last this story I've so longed to tell you—at last I can put this story in your hands. Now it is your responsibility to pass on to the next generation, so people will know the truth about Sarah and Hagar.

"And more!" she said. "Now you too can look beyond the world of jealousy and competition. You can ask yourself whether we must forever live according to the tale you learned in school—or has the time begun to come when women can shape the world together, as Hagar and Sarah tried to do."

Now, according to my mother, through all the generations this story has been passed on from woman to woman—to daughter, to niece, to granddaughter, to sister, to cousin. Never to men.

Yet now I have told it where men can also hear. For perhaps, at last, women and men together can learn from the story.

ABOUT THE AUTHORS

Joan Chittister, OSB, has been one of the Catholic Church's key visionary voices and spiritual leaders for more than thirty years. A Benedictine Sister of Erie, Pennsylvania, Chittister is an award-winning and best-selling author and a well-known international lecturer on behalf of peace, human rights, women's issues, and contemporary religious life and spirituality. Her recent books include *Scarred by Struggle, Transformed by Hope* and *Called to Question.*

Murshid Saadi Shakur Chishti (Neil Douglas-Klotz) is a world-renowned scholar in religious studies, spirituality, and psychology. He is the director of the Edinburgh Institute for Advanced Learning in Scotland, cofounder of the Edinburgh Festival of Middle Eastern Spirituality and Peace, and the author of many books, including *The Sufi Book of Life.*

Rabbi Arthur Waskow is the founder and director of The Shalom Center in Philadelphia, Pennsylvania, a prophetic voice in Jewish, multireligious, and American life that brings ancient and modern wisdom to bear on seeking peace, pursuing justice, healing the earth, and celebrating community. *Newsweek* recently named him one of the fifty most influential American rabbis, while the *Forward* named him one of the "Forward Fifty," among creative and effective American Jews. Waskow's books include *Godwrestling —Round 2*, *Seasons of Our Joy*, and *Down-to-Earth Judaism*.

Karen Armstrong is the best-selling author of *A History of God*, *Islam: A Short History*, and *The Battle for God*, among other books.